Wounded For Us

Scriptural Cures
For Our Wounds:
Lenten/Easter Resources

C. David Hogsett

CSS Publishing Company, Inc., Lima, Ohio

WOUNDED FOR US

Copyright © 2006 by
CSS Publishing Company, Inc.
Lima, Ohio

All rights reserved. No part of this publication may be reproduced in any manner whatsoever without the prior permission of the publisher, except in the case of brief quotations embodied in critical articles and reviews. Inquiries should be addressed to: Permissions, CSS Publishing Company, Inc., 517 South Main Street, Lima, Ohio 45804.

Scripture quotations are from the *New Revised Standard Version of the Bible*, copyright 1989 by the Division of Christian Education of the National Council of the Churches of Christ in the USA. Used by permission.

Library of Congress Cataloging-in-Publication Data

Hogsett, C. David.
   Wounded for us : scriptural cures for our wounds : Lenten/Easter resources / C. David Hogsett.
     p. cm.
   ISBN 0-7880-2391-8 (perfect bound : alk. paper)
   1. Lent—Prayer-books and devotions—English. 2. Easter—Prayer-books and devotions—English. 3. United Methodist Church (U.S.)—Prayer-books and devotions—English. 4. Worship programs. I. Title.
BV85.H635 2005
242'.34—dc22

                                        2005026664

For more information about CSS Publishing Company resources, visit our website at www.csspub.com or email us at custserv@csspub.com or call (800) 241-4056.

Cover design by Chris Patton
ISBN 0-7880-2391-8   PRINTED IN U.S.A.

To the
Crescent Avenue United Methodist Church,
the Trinity Church United Methodist,
and the East Noble Ministerial Association
who made it possible for
Wounded For Us
to become a reality

Table Of Contents

Preface	7
Introduction	9
Ash Wednesday	13
Worship Service	15
First Five Sundays In Lent	19
Worship Service	22
First Sunday In Lent	
Bulletin Insert	26
Sermon	27
Wounded In Our Thoughts	
Second Sunday In Lent	
Bulletin Insert	33
Sermon	34
Wounded In Our Spirit And Emotions	
Third Sunday In Lent	
Bulletin Insert	39
Sermon	40
Wounded In Our Hopes And Dreams	
Fourth Sunday In Lent	
Bulletin Insert	45
Sermon	46
Wounded In Our Relationships	
Fifth Sunday In Lent	
Bulletin Insert	52
Sermon	53
Wounded In Our Actions	
Palm Sunday	59
Worship Service One — Palm Sunday	61
Bulletin Insert	63
Sermon	64
A City In Turmoil	

Worship Service Two — Palm/Passion Sunday	68
Selected Scripture Readings	71
Maundy Thursday	75
Worship Service	78
Good Friday	81
Tenebrae Worship Service	83
Community Worship Service	87
Easter Sunday	93
Worship Service	94
Bulletin Insert	97
Sermon	99
Healed	
Visuals	103
Candles	103
Display	104
Handouts	104
Bulletins	105

Preface

Shortly after my appointment in June of 1990 to the Crescent Avenue United Methodist Church, in Fort Wayne, Indiana, while taking a tour of the facilities I noticed that engraved on the reredos of the altar were what appeared to be five Maltese crosses. I thought it somewhat unusual for a United Methodist Church but did not give it much more thought. It was only later that I learned of their significance.

For more than twenty years, a group of pastors from the North Indiana Conference of the United Methodist Church have been meeting three times a year with the Reverend Leonard Sweet for what the conference has titled "Great Books Seminar." If truth be known, some of the books that we have read have not been all that great. As a part of the November seminar following my starting of ministry at Crescent, Len shared with us his update of the traditional five wounds of Christ. As he was speaking, I thought of the five crosses on the altar at Crescent Avenue.

At the next meeting of the Crescent Avenue United Methodist Church's worship committee I explained what I learned at the Sweet seminar and suggested that we incorporate the five crosses on Crescent's altar as a part of the church's Lenten observance for the following year. The suggestion was made to place a votive candle in front of each of the crosses, one to be lit each Sunday of the first five Sundays in Lent to represent a particular wound of Jesus. The genesis for the materials in this book grew out of this emphasis. The following year the church replaced the votive candles with a Lenten wreath that had additional candles for Palm Sunday and Good Friday. In addition, rather than lighting a candle each week, one was extinguished.

Several years ago the local ministerial association used the five wounds as the framework for their Good Friday Service. A minister was assigned for each of the wounds to give a five-minute meditation. The liturgy from the first five Sundays of the Crescent Avenue's Lenten services was reduced into a single, one-hour service.

Trinity Church United Methodist in Kendallville, Indiana, used *Wounded For Us* for their 2004 Lenten emphasis, with the concept of the five wounds. A service for Maundy Thursday, as well as material for Easter Sunday, was added. Also, the Lenten wreath was transformed into an Easter wreath to be used during the season of Eastertide.

These materials that focus on the five wounds of Christ continue to evolve. Hopefully as your church uses them they will add to the ongoing recapturing of a most important part of our Christian tradition.

A word of thanks to the worship committees of the Crescent Avenue United Methodist Church in Fort Wayne, Indiana, and Trinity Church United Methodist in Kendallville, Indiana, for their input, sharing, and hard work that helped to make this book possible. Appreciation to the Reverend Leonard Sweet who connected for me the five crosses on the altar of Crescent Avenue United Methodist Church and the five wounds of Christ that sparked the development of this special Lenten emphasis. I am grateful to the Reverend Stan Kessler, a Presbyterian pastor here in Kendallville; my wife, Diane; and to Ruth Hougland who have spent many hours reading, editing, and revising my work.

Introduction

During the Middle Ages, there developed in the Roman Catholic Church a devotion to the five sacred wounds of Christ. Over time, preference was given to Christ being wounded in the side with the spear over the nails in his hands and feet. This gradually led to the cult of the Sacred Heart of Jesus that spawned the Sacred Heart of Mary. Prayers by such saints as Saint Clare of Assisi were written in honor of the sacred wounds. In southern Germany, a practice developed in the fourteenth century of offering fifteen *Pater Nosters* each day, three for each of the five wounds. Also, during the fourteenth century the monastery of Fritzlar, Thuringia, held a feast in honor of the wounds. In today's Roman Catholic mass, you will find a remnant of this devotion to the five wounds by the five signs of the cross immediately preceding and then following the consecration of the elements.

As was made evident by the widespread interest in Mel Gibson's movie, *The Passion Of The Christ*, there would once again seem to be a revival of interest in the wounds of Christ. Some have suggested that a possible explanation for this is that many today, especially those under the age of thirty, see themselves as being wounded. A growing number of Americans find it is easier to identify with the wounded Jesus rather than with the risen Christ. In the broken body of our Lord on the cross, people are able to see re-presented the brokenness in their own lives. In the crucifixion, the Son of Man is wounded for us.

While the place for many today to begin their walk with Jesus is Good Friday, the journey is only completed on Easter. As a consequence of his crucifixion, Jesus is not only able to identify with the places where people today are wounded, he is able to bring them reconciliation, resurrection, and new life. If you have not been feeling well for some time and have not known the reason, there is a sense of relief when you are finally able to name the illness. However, it is when a doctor is able to prescribe a cure that works that one is liberated from his or her illness. Easter has the potential to bring the same liberation for the places where we may be wounded.

Wounded For Us is a comprehensive Lenten emphasis that begins with the places where we find ourselves wounded, examines them in light of the five wounds of Christ, and then explores how Christ's resurrection can be a cure for the places where we are hurting. Included are worship materials for Ash Wednesday, the first five Sundays in Lent, Palm Sunday (the sixth Sunday in Lent), Maundy Thursday, Good Friday, and Easter. Suggestions are given for visuals that might be used with the program.

The traditional five wounds of feet (two), hands (two), and side (one) have been expanded to include head and back. Christ being wounded on his head by the crown of thorns is related to how we are wounded in our thoughts. Being wounded in our spirit and emotions is associated with our Lord being pierced in the side. The scourging on the back corresponds to the places in our lives where we are wounded in our hopes and dreams. The nails in Christ's hands are a reminder of how we are wounded in our relationships; the nails in his feet of how we are wounded in our actions.

To introduce the theme of *Wounded For Us*, an Ash Wednesday service has been provided. On this first day of Lent we are once again made aware of the transitory nature of our existence and our propensity to be wounded as a part of our mortality. The imposition of the ashes on the forehead reminds us of the places in our lives where we are broken and in need of healing and reconciliation. As a part of the service, the five wounds of Christ and the corresponding places in our lives where we may be wounded are introduced. This is also an opportunity to introduce the chosen arrangements for the candles that will be extinguished as a part of the Lenten services.

At the heart of *Wounded For Us* are the first five Sundays in Lent. This is a time for the people to take an honest look at their lives to see where they are wounded. In addition to a general outline for the services and propers for specific Sundays, sermon notes are provided each week to assist the people in understanding each of the wounds and to guide them in their reflection following the sermon. To help the pastor prepare a message for each of the wounds, a sermon is given. These are intended to be general outlines to stimulate thinking, not to be taken verbatim.

It has become customary to observe the sixth Sunday in Lent as Palm/Passion Sunday. *Wounded For Us* focuses just on Palm Sunday, assuming the passion aspects of Holy Week will be cared for by the Maundy Thursday and Good Friday services. As Jesus rides down the Mount of Olives and across the Kidron Valley, he enters a city in turmoil. The first five Sundays in Lent have examined how we are wounded individually. Palm Sunday is a time to have a look at how we are wounded corporately.

Using one of the narratives from one of the synoptic gospels on Maundy Thursday, the people are invited to travel with Jesus and his disciples from the preparations for the Last Supper to when they depart for the Garden of Gethsemane. Included in the service are elements from the Jewish Passover. Special emphasis is given to Jesus' breaking of the bread. The people are invited to name the place or places in their lives where they are broken, where they are wounded, where they need to experience the healing power of Jesus.

Two resources are provided for Good Friday. One has as its target a community Good Friday service where various pastors are invited to participate. This service is self-contained, not assuming that those attending have been involved in the other aspects of *Wounded For Us*. The second resource is an adaptation of the traditional Tenebrae service especially for this program. It could also be used as a community service.

Easter Sunday is a time to claim and celebrate the working of the crucified and resurrected Christ, to bring about the healing of our wounds. The black or purple candles of Lent are replaced with white candles of resurrection. The *Wounded For Us* program ends with Easter, but a church may choose to continue its celebration of Christ healing our wounds by continuing to light the Easter wreath during the whole of the Eastertide season.

A section has been provided with suggestions for visuals that might be used as a part of this emphasis. Ideas will be given on how to display the candles that are to be extinguished each Sunday, including several suggestions for Lenten wreaths. Some churches may want to have a changing or growing display that might include a crown of thorns, a whip, nails, and a spear.

The good news of the Christian gospel is that on the cross Jesus died to set us free from bonds of sin and death, to do for us what we are unable to do for ourselves, to take upon himself the places in our lives where we are wounded so that through the power of God demonstrated in his resurrection, he might bring about healing, wholeness, new life, and resurrection. *Wounded For Us* is an opportunity for you and your church together to examine the places where you are hurting to allow Jesus to take our wounds upon himself, and to experience the power of God working through you to bring about health and regeneration. May God richly bless you and move in your midst in a powerful way as you explore what it means that Jesus was wounded for you.

Ash Wednesday

For a while, as a child, my family lived over the hardware store that my father owned. My front yard was the main street of New Brighten, Pennsylvania, with an alley being my backyard. One Wednesday in March, I was exploring my domain when I began to notice people with something black on their foreheads. Had a new and strange disease broken out that caused these affectations? Since the Methodist church that my family attended did not observe Ash Wednesday, I was not familiar with the tradition of the imposition of ashes on Ash Wednesday.

The observance of Ash Wednesday goes back to at least the tenth century, marking a transition from doing formal penance by individuals during the Lenten season to a general time of penitential devotion by all. The ashes produced by the burning of the palms from the previous year's Palm Sunday were a reminder to the worshipers of their mortality, from dust we come and to dust we shall return. The service was also intended to be a call to faithfulness to the gospel.

Ash Wednesday affords a fit setting to introduce *Wounded For Us*. An important aspect of our mortality is our being wounded in our thoughts, our spirit and emotions, our hopes and dreams, our relationships, and our actions. When as a child I saw for the first time people with crosses on their foreheads, I wondered if there was an outbreak of a contagious illness. Ash Wednesday affirms there is. It is a condition that is a result of our being born and it has affected all of society.

The following Ash Wednesday service is the one that was used by the Crescent Avenue United Methodist Church in its observance of the five wounds of Christ. It incorporated the presentation of five votive candles that were placed in front of the five crosses on the reredos of the church's altar. Churches using *Wounded For Us* will want to adjust the presentation section of this service to correspond with the number of candles they will be using in their observance and how they are to be displayed.

The prayer that follows the greeting should have Ash Wednesday as its theme. United Methodists may want to use the prayer that is found on page 353 of *The United Methodist Hymnal*. The theme for the sermon or meditation will be dependent upon a particular church's traditions and understanding of Ash Wednesday, upon how a church chooses to incorporate *Wounded For Us* as a part of their Lenten observance, and upon which direction the pastor of the church decides to approach the sermons for the Sundays of Lent and Easter.

As mentioned earlier, the Crescent Avenue's Ash Wednesday service incorporates the presentation of five votive candles. The service has made provision for the presentation of a Palm Sunday candle and a Good Friday candle. As a verse of "Were You There?" is sung, a votive candle is brought forward and placed in front of one of the five candles on the altar, followed by a scripture reading. For this program, three additional verses of "Were You There?" have been written: "Were you there when they crowned him with the thorns?" "Were you there when they scourged him on the back?" and "Were you there when he rode into Jerusalem?"

After all of the candles have been presented, it is suggested that someone make a short presentation that relates the candles, our being wounded, and ashes as a symbol of our mortality. In the service, this is followed by the song "Ashes," written by Tom Conry for North American Liturgy Resource and is found in *Gather* (GIA Publications, Inc.) on page 173. During the singing of this song, the Lenten candles are lit. Instead of having a congregational song at this point, an anthem or special music may be used.

For the imposition of ashes, each church will want to follow their normal customs and practices. The Prayer For The Ashes and the words for the imposition of the ashes have been adapted for *Wounded For Us*. The prayer following the imposition should be one in keeping with the church's conventional observance of Ash Wednesday.

Worship Service

Ash Wednesday

Prelude

Greeting   1 Peter 2:24
    On the cross Christ bore our sins
    So that we might live for righteousness
    By his wounds
    We can be healed.

Opening Prayer

Lenten Hymn   "Lord, Who Throughout These Forty Days"

Old Testament Lesson   Isaiah 53:1-12

Reading From The Psalter   Psalm 51:1-17

Epistle Lesson   Hebrews 4:14-16; 5:7-9

Gospel Hymn   "O Sacred Head, Now Wounded"

Gospel Lesson   Matthew 16:21-28

Sermon   "Wounded For Us"

                      Presentation Of The Five Candles
Candle One: Christ Wounded On The Head
    Hymn   "Were You There?"
    "Were you there when they crowned him with the thorns?"
    Scripture   Matthew 27:27-31

Candle Two: Christ Pierced In The Side
    Hymn   "Were You There?"
      "Were you there when they pierced him in the side?"
    Scripture   John 19:33, 34

Candle Three: Christ Scourged On The Back
    Hymn   "Were You There?"
      "Were you there when they scourged him on the back?"
    Scripture   Matthew 27:26

Candle Four: Christ Wounded On His Hands
    Hymn   "Were You There?"
      "Were you there when they nailed him to the tree?"
    Scripture   Matthew 27:35-37

Candle Five: Christ Wounded On His Feet
    Hymn   "Were You There?"
      "Were you there when they nailed him to the tree?"
    Scripture   John 19:16-18

Palm Sunday Candle
    Hymn   "Were You There?"
      "Were you there when he rode into Jerusalem?"
    Scripture   Matthew 21:1-11

Good Friday Candle
    Hymn   "Were You There?"
      "Were you there when they crucified my Lord?"
    Scripture   Mark 15:25-39

Imposition Of Ashes
Ashes As A Symbol Of Our Being Wounded

Song   "Ashes"
    (Lighting of the Lenten candles)

Thanksgiving Over The Ashes
Almighty God, you formed us out of the dust of the earth and breathed into us the breath of life.

Grant that these ashes may be to us a symbol of our mortality, of our failures, and of the places in our lives where we are wounded, so that we may remember that only by your gracious gift and the sacrifice of your Son can healing and wholeness take place.

Through Jesus Christ our Savior. Amen.

Imposition Of Ashes
Repent, and believe the good news that on the cross Christ was wounded for the places in our lives where we are wounded.

Prayer

The Peace

Closing Hymn   "Pass Me Not, O Gentle Savior"

Benediction

Postlude

First Five Sundays In Lent

The topic of discussion for the morning was the church year. I had just shared with the members of the 2001 Confirmation Class that Ash Wednesday falls forty days before Easter and Christ's ascension forty days after. As usually happens, one of the confirmands was quick to point out that there were actually 46 days between Ash Wednesday and Easter. Why the discrepancy? I explained to the class that it is because we do not count the Sundays since they are little Easters.

As the members of a congregation examine the areas of their lives where they are wounded, the six Sundays in Lent (the first five Sundays plus Palm Sunday) provide an opportunity to experience not only the healing power of Christ's death on the cross, but also his victory on Easter. Each Sunday can become a little Easter. The climax of these services is the extinguishing of a Lenten candle to represent on the one hand a place where Christ was wounded, and on the other how the worshipers can appropriate the redemptive power of Christ's wounds to effect healing where they are wounded.

The first six services begin with a Call To Worship based on Hebrews 4:14-16. In this text, Jesus is pictured as our great high priest who is able to sympathize with our wounds (weakness) because he has been tested in the same way we have. As a consequence of Christ's intimacy with our afflictions, we can boldly approach the throne of grace with the assurance that we will find a receptive ear as well as one who is able to bring about forgiveness, healing, redemption, and reconciliation.

Note: the Greeting from the Ash Wednesday service based on 1 Peter 2:24 may be used in place of this Call To Worship.

The point in the service where the specific emphasis for the day is introduced is with the reading of the scriptures. For each Sunday, three texts are suggested: an Old Testament, an Epistle, and a Gospel. The Old Testament Readings are from those sections of Isaiah that describe the Messiah as the suffering servant. The Epistle Lessons come from the book of James. An attempt has been made to correlate these passages with the theme for each day. The wound for a specific Sunday is introduced with the reading of the Gospel Lesson.

A sermon is included for each of the first five Sundays in Lent. The primary thrust of these messages is to examine the ways in which we are wounded in our thoughts, our hopes and dreams, our emotions and our spirit, our relationships, and our actions. In most instances, the source of our wounds is ourselves. Either intentionally or unintentionally, by our choices and actions, we are the cause of our own injury. Another approach would be to focus on how we are wounded because of outside forces. An example of such an approach would be the suggested sermon for Palm Sunday.

The final portion of each message describes how we can appropriate the redemptive power of Jesus' death on the cross to heal our wounds. In the "Sermon Notes" this is referred to as the "Cure." Each cure takes the form of a scripture reading. Each sermon suggests an action plan of how we can apply the cure to our lives. In light of the popularity of the movie, *The Passion Of The Christ*, one might choose to give more emphasis in these sermons to each of the specific wounds.

The first five sermons, as well as the other sermons in this material, are intended to be a guide for the preacher as he or she prepares a message that is relevant to his or her situation. While a pastor may want to use the general outline for each message, the sermons are not written to be used verbatim. In fact, more material is included than could possibly be used for any one Sunday. What is provided are possibilities to stimulate a pastor's thinking. Hopefully they might spark other illustrations on the part of the person preparing a specific sermon.

With each message, a sermon outline is included. It should be given as bulletin insert. This summary functions in two ways. First, it serves as a guide for the congregation to follow as they listen to the sermon. Second, following the sermon, it is a framework for the worshipers to use as they meditate on the places in their lives where they are wounded. In these services, the order of the wounds is dictated by the places where we are wounded: from the inside to outward actions. On Good Friday, we return to the order in which

Jesus was wounded. The final section of each of these outlines suggests a cure that can be used in the development of an action plan for the week to come.

A "Hymn Of Preparation" and "Hymn Of Going" are suggested with each of the sample sermons. They have been selected to reinforce the sermon. A "Sending Forth" for each Sunday has also been included. They are intended to buttress the action plan that has been suggested in the sermon.

Following the sermon, two verses of "Were You There?" are sung. The first verse is always the same with the second verse picking up on the wound for the day. Since the hymn as published does not have verses that refer to Jesus being flogged or having the crown of thorns placed on his head, special stanzas have been written for these two Sundays. During the singing of the second verse, a Lenten candle is extinguished.

The general outline for the prayer following the Lenten hymn, "Were You There?" is the same. Each week the appropriate candle number, the wound, and description of where we are wounded is inserted. The congregational-sung benediction, verses 1 and 3 of "Near The Cross," is the same for the six Sundays in Lent.

The service that follows is a composite of several used by the author at two different churches. Each church where this program is used will want to adapt this outline to their general worship format. The celebration of the Lord's Supper is not incorporated in this service. Suggestions concerning this are included in the section having to do with Maundy Thursday.

Worship Service

First Five Sundays In Lent

Prelude

Call To Worship ~~Hebrews 4:14-16~~
Since, then, we have a great high priest who has passed through the heavens, Jesus, the Son of God,
let us hold fast to our confession.
For we do not have a high priest who is unable to sympathize with our weaknesses,
but we have one who in every respect has been tested as we are, yet without sin.
Let us therefore approach the throne of grace with boldness,
so that we may receive mercy and find grace to help in time of need.

Hymn Of Gathering

Greeting One Another

Welcome Of Guests

Announcements

Morning Prayers

Anthem

Scripture Readings
　Week One: Isaiah 50:4-9; James 3:1-12; Matthew 27:27-31
　Week Two: Isaiah 42:1-4; James 3:13-18; John 19:33-34
　Week Three: Isaiah 40:1-11; James 4:13-17; Matthew 27:26
　Week Four: Isaiah 52:13—53:3; James 4:1-10; Matthew 27:35-37
　Week Five: Isaiah 53:4-9; James 1:22-25; John 19:16-18

Gospel Lesson Wounds
    Week One: On the head
    Week Two: In the side
    Week Three: On the back
    Week Four: On the hands
    Week Five: On the feet

Offering

Hymn Of Preparation
    Week One: "Breathe On Me, Breath Of God"
    Week Two: "What A Friend We Have In Jesus"
    Week Three: "My Hope Is Built"
    Week Four: "In The Garden"
    Week Five: "Savior, Like A Shepherd Lead Us"

Sermon
    Week One: "Wounded In Our Thoughts"
    Week Two: "Wounded In Our Spirit And Emotions"
    Week Three: "Wounded In Our Hopes And Dreams"
    Week Four: "Wounded In Our Relationships"
    Week Five: "Wounded In Our Actions"

Lenten Hymn   "Were You There?"
(Extinguish one Lenten candle each week after singing these verses)
    Week One: Verse 1 and "Were you there when they crowned him with the thorns?"
    Week Two: Verse 1 and "Were you there when they pierced him in the side?"
    Week Three: Verse 1 and "Were you there when they scourged him on the back?"
    Week Four: Verse 1 and "Were you there when they nailed him to the tree?"
    Week Five: Verse 1 and "Were you there when they nailed him to the tree?"

Prayer

Week One: Our Father, we have extinguished our first Lenten candle as a reminder that Jesus was wounded on the head by a crown of thorns. It is also a symbol of the places in our lives where we are wounded because of our own thoughts. Take upon yourself our wounds that you might redeem and resurrect them, setting us free for a life of everlasting joy and peace. Amen.

Week Two: Our Father, we have extinguished our second Lenten candle as a reminder that Jesus was wounded in the side with a spear. It is also a symbol of the places in our lives where we are wounded in our spirit and our emotions. Take upon yourself our wounds that you might redeem and resurrect them, setting us free for a life of everlasting joy and peace. Amen.

Week Three: Our Father, we have extinguished our third Lenten candle as a reminder that Jesus was wounded on the back with a whip. It is also a symbol of the places in our lives where we are wounded in our hopes and dreams. Take upon yourself our wounds that you might redeem and resurrect them, setting us free for a life of everlasting joy and peace. Amen.

Week Four: Our Father, we have extinguished our fourth Lenten candle as a reminder that Jesus was wounded on the hands with nails. It is also a symbol of the places in our lives where we are wounded in our relationships. Take upon yourself our wounds that you might redeem and resurrect them, setting us free for a life of everlasting joy and peace. Amen.

Week Five: Our Father, we have extinguished our fifth Lenten candle as a reminder that Jesus was wounded on the feet with nails. It is also a symbol of the places in our lives where we are wounded in our actions. Take upon yourself our wounds that you might redeem and resurrect them, setting us free for a life of everlasting joy and peace. Amen.

Hymn Of Going

Week One: "Be Thou My Vision"
Week Two: "Precious Name"
Week Three: "Spirit Of The Living God"
Week Four: "Trust And Obey"
Week Five: "Love Divine, All Loves Excelling"

Sending Forth
Week One: In this coming week, be transformed by the renewing of your minds so that you might discern what is the will of God — what is good and acceptable and perfect. Amen.

Week Two: In this coming week, be transformed by giving to Jesus the places in your life where you are wounded in your emotions and spirit that he might take them upon himself and make your burdens light. Amen.

Week Three: In this coming week, be transformed by opening yourself to the living Christ that he might interpret your dreams and open the door of your future hopes. Amen.

Week Four: In this coming week, be transformed by allowing the Spirit of Christ to be alive in the places in your life where you walk through the dark valleys because of broken relationships. Amen.

Week Five: In this coming week, be transformed by reaching out to Jesus that he might raise you from the places you would sink. Amen.

Congregational Benediction   "Near The Cross" (vv. 1, 3)

Jesus, keep me near the cross; there a precious fountain, free to all, a healing stream, flows from Calvary's mountain. In the cross, in the cross, be my glory ever, till my raptured soul shall find rest beyond the river.

Near the cross! O Lamb of God, bring its scenes before me; help me walk from day to day with its shadows o'er me. In the cross, in the cross, be my glory ever, till my raptured soul shall find rest beyond the river.

Postlude

Bulletin Insert

First Sunday In Lent

Wounded In Our Thoughts

Isaiah 50:4-9
James 3:1-12
Matthew 27:27-31

Sermon Notes

Causes
  Bad tapes (bad programs)
  Poor self-image
  Self-centeredness (pride)
  Bad information
  Rut thinking (not open to *new* information)
  Prejudice
  Negative input

Cure
  Do not be conformed to this world, but be transformed by the renewing of your minds, so that you may discern what is the will of God — what is good and acceptable and perfect.
  — Romans 12:2

Sermon

Wounded In Our Thoughts
Isaiah 50:4-9; James 3:1-12; Matthew 27:27-31

(The sermon begins with illustrations of people whose identities are shaped by their self-image. Below you will find examples that were used for the week of February 29, 2004. The pastor may want to use illustrations that are more current and relevant to his or her congregation.)

A suicide bomber detonated an explosive-packed vehicle outside of an Iraqi police station in a Kurdish neighborhood in Kirkuk, killing at least fifteen people and wounding 45 others.

Only four percent of Amish men are obese versus 31 percent of non-Amish men. Why? In an experiment, 100 adults in an Amish farming community in southern Ontario wore pedometers and logged their physical activity for a week. The men reported ten hours of vigorous work a week and averaged 18,425 steps a day. All told, they engaged in six times as much physical activity as did their "modern" counterparts (*Time*, February 9, 2004).

Enrollment at Azusa Pacific University (A.P.U.), the second largest evangelical Christian college with an enrollment of 8,200, has risen 27 percent since 1997. "Young people want to know something bigger than themselves," says senior Marcus Robinson, 24 (*Time*, February 2, 2004).

For several months, motorists in the Columbus, Ohio, area have been victims of a sniper who so far has killed one lady. From the information which has been released, it would appear that the white, male shooter just gets his kicks out of shooting at cars passing him on the interstate.

A woman pleads guilty to setting fire to the trailer in which her three children were sleeping. In a letter filed with the court she states: "The sooner I can get bonded out then I can take on my motherly responsibilities of my young children. My children are everything to me."

An Islamic terrorist, Amish men, students attending an evangelical Christian college, the Columbus sniper, and a mother who sets her trailer on fire: what do these six examples have in common? Each of these individuals or groups acted on the content of their minds. Their "take" on reality informs their decision, dictates their priorities, and frames their response to their environment.

This observation is not only true for the above six examples, it is true for each of us. Our worldview, formed over many years of experience, input, and evaluation, predisposes us to think, observe, reason, and act in predetermined ways. Much of what we do, how we see our world, and our understanding of reality is based on the content of our minds. On the whole it is good content and serves us well. But we can also be wounded in our thoughts, we can have content which is unhealthy, non-productive, and which continually gets us into trouble.

Bad Tapes (Bad Programs)

In the '70s, Thomas Harris made "Transactional Analysis" a part of the American vocabulary with the publishing of his book, *I'm OK — You're OK*. For Harris we all have inside our human consciousness tapes, many of which go back to our earliest days and months, which begin to play when we find ourselves confronted by a challenge or a threat, called upon to perform a particular task, or presented with a new or novel situation. They form the basis of our conditioned response to our environment. Fortunately, most of the time these tapes serve us well. However, there may be some whose content habitually gets us into trouble. When one of them begins to play, we might well say to ourselves, "Well, I've done it again."

I suspect if Harris were writing his book today, instead of using the imagery of tapes, he might well use computer programs. Our brain is a computer filled with programs that allow us to function. For the most part they perform without a hitch. However, when they have been improperly installed, have become corrupt, or have been invaded by a virus, they can cause great harm and distress.

What happens to your computer when it has a bad program or one that has become corrupt or has a virus? It does not work well. And you get very frustrated, very upset, and very angry, trying to correct the problem. So it is with us when one of the programs in our head has become faulty, or has become wounded.

Poor Self-image

For Thomas Harris, a tape that is common for a majority of Americans is "I'm not okay, you're okay." Most of us suffer from a poor self-image. Somehow no matter how much we do, how much we accomplish, how much people affirm us, we still do not feel worthy. We think to ourselves, "If people only really knew me, they would think differently about me. They would never like me." Somehow we don't quite measure up. It doesn't seem to matter how much good we do, how much we accomplish, or how much people say how wonderful we are, we still do not feel good about ourselves.

Self-centeredness (Pride)

The opposite of a poor self-image is self-centeredness. Here the faulty tape is "I'm okay, everyone else is not okay." The scriptures identify this as the sin of pride. No one else can do things as well as I can, have ideas as good as I have, or is as worthy of praise as I am. In fact, I am a superior individual. The content of the mind of a person who suffers from self-centeredness and pride is filled with the pronoun "I." "I think." "I want." "I believe." It goes on and on and on.

Bad Information

Every once in a while, I discover that a bit of information that I was sure was absolutely true turns out to be inaccurate. Usually they have to do with my take on past events. Fortunately, these bad bits of information don't make much difference in the big scheme of things. When they are discovered, it is good to get them corrected. There are those that can cause serious harm. Here it is imperative that they be identified and quickly corrected.

Rut Thinking (Not Open To New Information)

Much of the time I practice what I call "rut thinking." I have this entrenched sorting system that very quickly categorizes each new bit of information and deposits it into well-established pigeonholes. Without such a system I would go crazy making decisions of where to put every new fact. The problem arises when something novel makes its way into my sorting program, is not recognized, and is disposed of in the same old place. There are those times when it is important to get out of one's rut and take a fresh look at things.

Prejudice

One of the ruts that does not serve us well is pigeonholing people by a particular group with which they are associated. We call this prejudice. We have our set ideas of just what a Republican or a Democrat is, of what a person who belongs to a particular nationality or race is like, of what certain trigger words mean for us. We see the world through our stereotypes of it. These preconceptions prevent us from seeing people as individuals. Instead, we see them as categories.

Negative Input

In the world of computers is the axiom: "Garbage in, garbage out." If one only fills his or her mind with negative, depressing, unhealthy, and immoral information, one should not be surprised when his or her picture of the world is negative, depressing, unhealthy, and immoral. From the home where we live, to the place where we work, to what we watch on television, to the friends we have, to how we occupy our free time, we are filling our minds with information. Taken together, this database colors how we see and experience life.

Jesus Takes Our Bad Tapes Upon Himself

The good news is that on the cross, Jesus takes the bad tapes and programs that influence our thinking upon himself, then redeems and transforms them into something new. In the opening of his letter to the Corinthians Paul writes: "For the message about the cross is foolishness to those who are perishing, but to us who are being saved it is the power of God.... For Jews demand signs and Greeks desire wisdom, but we proclaim Christ crucified, a stumbling block to Jews and foolishness to Gentiles, but to those who are called, both Jews and Greeks, Christ is the power of God and the wisdom of God. For God's foolishness is wiser than human wisdom, and God's weakness is stronger than human strength" (1 Corinthians 1:18, 22-25).

On the cross Jesus takes upon himself our tapes of poor self-image and affirms us to be a person of worth and value.

On the cross Jesus takes upon himself our tapes of self-centeredness and pride and helps us to take the role of a servant.

On the cross Jesus takes upon himself our tapes that have bad information and assists us to identify it and then correct it.

On the cross Jesus takes upon himself our tapes that have become routine and helps us to see the new and the novel.

On the cross Jesus takes upon himself our tapes of prejudice and allows us to see people with fresh eyes, not as categories.

On the cross Jesus takes upon himself our tapes that are filled with garbage and fills them with something beautiful.

Plan Of Action

As Paul moves in his letter to the Romans from his theological section to his more practical section he invites his readers "not to be conformed to this world, but [to] be transformed by the renewing of [their] minds, so that [they] may discern what is the will of God — what is good and acceptable and perfect" (Romans 12:2). This morning as we begin this Lenten season I would invite all of us to be transformed by the renewing of the content of our minds. In just a few minutes you will be invited to examine the content of your mind to discover the places where you may be wounded. Then we will be praying together that Christ may take upon himself these wounds, redeeming them, and bringing about resurrection and new life.

As we are taking stock of the content of our minds, it may not be readily apparent the places where we are wounded. Sometimes they are so subtle and have become so much a part of the fabric of our lives that they have become second nature to us. During this Lenten season we need to be in prayer that Jesus would help us to identify the places where we are wounded in our thinking, places that need transformation.

To help with your examination of the content of your minds, you will find a bulletin insert that has listed each of the seven areas mentioned this morning. You may want to begin your time of meditation by asking yourself, "In which of these areas am I wounded?" When you have made your list, you may find it helpful to choose one that you want to give to Christ so that he might work during this Lenten season to bring about redemption and resurrection.

Let us all now be in a period of self-examination and reflection.

Bulletin Insert

Second Sunday In Lent

Wounded In Our Spirit And Emotions

Isaiah 42:1-4
James 3:13-18
John 19:33-34

Sermon Notes

Causes
    Emotions
        Unresolved anger
        Unresolved guilt
        Shame
        Bitterness
        Out of control
        Other
    Spirit
        Constantly beaten down
        Helplessness
        Hopelessness
        Other

Cure

Come to me, all you that are weary and are carrying heavy burdens, and I will give you rest. Take my yoke upon you, and learn from me; for I am gentle and humble in heart, and you will find rest for your souls. For my yoke is easy, and my burden is light.   — Matthew 11:28-30

Sermon

Wounded In Our Spirit And Emotions
Isaiah 42:1-4; James 3:13-18; John 19:33-34

In his hymn "What A Friend We Have In Jesus," Joseph M. Scriven writes the haunting words: "O what peace we often forfeit, O what needless pain we bear, all because we do not carry everything to God in prayer." In the total context of the hymn, Scriven might well have written, "O what peace we often forfeit, O what needless pain we bear, all because we do not carry everything to **Jesus** in prayer." Joseph pictures Jesus as a mother who gently rocks and comforts her child and as a friend who shares and bears our sorrows, hears our prayers, and then carries them to God.

The third verse of "What A Friend We Have In Jesus" begins by asking the question: "Are we weak and heavy laden, cumbered with a load of cares?" Later it inquires, "Do thy friends despise, forsake thee?" Here we have the description of a person who is in danger of being broken in spirit and of being overwhelmed by his or her emotions. To those who are going through such dark days, Jesus says, "Come to me, all you that are weary and are carrying heavy burdens, and I will give you rest. Take my yoke upon you, and learn from me; for I am gentle and humble in heart, and you will find rest for your souls. For my yoke is easy, and my burden is light" (Matthew 11:28-30).

(The following illustration of a woman who is wounded in her emotions and spirit may be used next, or one of the preacher's own choosing can be substituted.)

Eve is a sixty-year-old married woman who is generous, giving, active in mission projects in her church, involved in a Bible study, prays regularly, and has a sweet countenance. Her husband, George, describes her as someone who would give you the shirt off her back. Eve would not appear to be a likely candidate for a person who is wounded in her emotions and spirit. Nevertheless, Eve is a woman who suffers extreme emotional and spiritual pain because of bitterness, self-blame, shame, unresolved anger, and guilt. Several times a month, the pain becomes so unbearable that medication is not even able to numb it.

Eve's parents divorced when she was in her early twenties. Because she was sympathetic to her father when he consulted with her, Eve blames herself for the separation. In spite of the divorce, Eve and her family continued to meet on Mondays to do gardening and other projects, just as if nothing had ever happened. This time together ended when Eve, George, and their three children moved out of state, far away from her extended family. This meant that her young children did not have the opportunity of spending time with their aunts and uncles, grandparents, and cousins.

When Eve's children were in junior and senior high school, George abandoned the family for three years, living in an RV because "of her yelling." Her children became involved with drugs during this time. As a struggling, single mother, she had thoughts of divorcing her husband and moving back to Indiana and her family. But she didn't, even though she believed that God told her to. In time, her husband moved back and the children moved out to start their own families.

When Eve's husband retired, the two of them moved back to Indiana to a modest home. Eve was still bitter and angry toward George, unable to forgive him for having abandoned the family and unable to forgive herself for not divorcing him. Recently, their divorced daughter with her two sons, the wife of one of the sons, and three children from this wife's previous marriage moved back to Indiana to get away from the husband/father. He had lost custody of the children because of drugs. They moved in with Eve and George, but Eve felt George did not welcome them and his attitude drove them out of the house after three weeks. Because of this, Eve feels shame, guilt, anger, bitterness. She feels hopeless, helpless, and powerless. She can't forgive George and she can't forgive herself. And yet the fear of being alone is even greater than her anger toward him.

Eve is a woman who is deeply wounded in spirit. She depends on her own good resolutions and willpower. As she reaches out to Jesus, she finds relief but then withdraws back to her wounded self. Old bad tapes about her self-worth and a medical, chemical imbalance block her path.

Oh, that Eve might taste God's compassion as his grace reaches out to her. God's mercy will not eradicate the wound, but it "soothes the soul and draws it forward to a hope that purifies and sets free!" (*The Wounded Heart*, by Dan Allender, Colorado Springs, Colorado: Nav Press, 1990, p. 263)

(What follows is an examination of the ways that Eve is wounded in spirit and emotions. If another example(s) is used, the preacher may wish to identify here the examples of wounds identified in the example or examples.)

Eve is wounded in her emotions in at least five ways: unresolved anger, unresolved guilt, bitterness, shame, and lack of control. Eve is angry at her parents for divorcing, at her husband for abandoning the family for three years, at her children for some of their behavior, and at herself. Rather than coming to terms and dealing with this anger, she has allowed it to fester, year after year. The longer it has gone unresolved, the more power it has in her life.

One of the forms that Eve's anger takes is guilt toward herself. Even though she has asked many times for God to forgive her, she has never really been able to forgive herself. She is not only wounded in her emotions and spirit, she is wounded in her thoughts. Eve suffers from the bad tape that says, "No matter how hard you try or what you may do, you are always going to be not okay."

Another way that Eve experiences a low self-esteem is a constant sense of shame. She is ashamed of her inferred part in her parent's divorce, of not having divorced George when he left, and of her perceived cause of much of her children's difficulties. Eve's shame is so great that she is convinced that God could never really forgive her. She is too great a sinner.

With this mixture of emotions swirling around inside her, is it any wonder that Eve is bitter about life? To meet her for the first time, you would never guess how deep this emotion runs, but it is exactly because she feels that it is unacceptable to express her bitterness, it has grown to have such a hold on her life.

On a regular basis her anger, her guilt, her shame, and her bitterness gang up and overwhelm Eve, making it difficult for her to function. Much of the time Eve is able to keep her emotions under control with pharmaceutical and talk therapy, but during these extreme times even those cannot provide relief.

The wounds that Eve has experienced in her emotions, over time, have beaten her down so that she has also become wounded in her spirit. After sixty years of unresolved anger, unresolved guilt, shame, and bitterness, Eve is coming to the end of her rope. She feels helpless and hopeless. One of Eve's tapes tells her that she is responsible for her parents, her husband, and her family. Experience has shown her that there is no way that she can live up to this unrealistic expectation. Is it any wonder that she feels helpless to affect in any positive way her life situation?

If the feeling of helplessness persists too long, it can lead to a sense of hopelessness. All that remains is a hope to endure. The possibility of experiencing joy, happiness, peace, and contentment has faded into the distant past. The goal becomes to just make it through another day.

This morning as we have listened to the story of Eve, perhaps we have seen described an aspect of her life that resonates with our own. Eve's story may have helped to sharpen the places where we may be wounded in spirit and emotions. Our pain may be like Eve's, similar to her anguish, or of a completely different nature. Her story, however, would invite all of us to examine our own soul to see where we may be wounded in our spirit and emotions.

This morning you are invited to bring to Jesus the places in your life where you are wounded in spirit and emotions. As the hymn, "What A Friend We Have In Jesus" suggests, "O what peace we often forfeit, O what needless pain we bear, all because we do not carry everything to [Jesus] in prayer." Using the sheet in the bulletin this morning you are encouraged to take an inventory of your life to see where you are wounded. Then you are invited to take your wounds to Jesus in prayer in order that he might redeem, resurrect, and bring about healing.

One of Eve's problems is that she is good at taking everything to Jesus in prayer. But she is also good at taking back what she had given to Jesus. A saying that was made popular in the '60s by the lay witness movement of the United Methodist Church was to "Let go, and let God." Like many of us, instead of letting go and letting God, Eve practices letting go and taking back. This morning I would invite each of us to examine our lives to discover those places that we may be wounded in spirit and emotions. Then let them go, and let Jesus do his work.

Bulletin Insert

Third Sunday In Lent

Wounded In Our Hopes And Dreams

Isaiah 40:4-11
James 4:13-17
Matthew 27:26

Sermon Notes

Cause
    Disciples after the crucifixion
        Reversals of fortune
        Outside forces
        Unrealistic hopes and dreams
    Other causes
        Changing stages of life
        Inability to adjust to other changing situations
        Criticism from others
        Repeated defeats
        Lack of hopes and dreams

Cure
The one of the two on the road to Emmaus replied, "But we had hoped that he was the one to redeem Israel and besides all this, it is now the third day since these things took place.... Then beginning with Moses and the prophets, (Jesus) interpreted to them the things about himself in all the scriptures."
                                              — Luke 24:21, 27

Sermon

Wounded In Our Hopes And Dreams
Isaiah 40:4-11; James 4:13-17; Matthew 27:26

Last Christmas, my brother, Art, gave me a copy of Studs Terkel's newest book, *Hope Dies Last*. It is a collection of interviews in which Terkel inquires concerning the place of hope in the lives of a variety of people who have taken an active part in the political arena of our country the last half of the twentieth century. The book is a chronicle of the importance of hope if a person is to face difficult circumstances, battle against overwhelming odds, and challenge prevailing ways of thinking. In his introduction, Studs notes: "As we enter the new millennium, hope appears to be an American attribute that has vanished for many, no matter what their class or condition in life."

Following the crucifixion of Jesus, hope would also seem to have vanished from the lives of his disciples and his followers. They were seriously wounded in their hope that Jesus was the Messiah and their dreams of the reign of God coming on earth. In Luke we read the story of two followers of Jesus who had been in Jerusalem for the Passover, had shared the excitement and raised expectations of Christ's presence, had learned of his death, and were now discouraged as they were on their way home to a town called Emmaus. When Jesus comes to walk with them, they share how they had hoped that this Jesus of Nazareth would be the long-expected Messiah. With his death, this hope and dream had been shattered. What was there left for which to live?

At least three things caused the two travelers to be wounded in their hopes and dreams: reversals of fortune, outside forces, and unrealistic hopes and dreams. First, in the early days of Jesus' ministry with all of its excitement and triumphs, it was easy to believe that he was the long-expected Messiah. However, when the crowds began to grow smaller, strong opposition started to surface, and Jesus himself talked about his mission ending on a cross, doubts began to grow as to the truth of their hope for the meaning of Jesus' coming. Going from a king riding into Jerusalem on Palm Sunday to a common criminal executed on a cross on Friday inflicted a severe blow to the travelers' hopes of who Jesus was.

Among the religious, political, economic, and social leaders, Jesus was not popular. They were out to shatter the hopes and dreams that were being created among the crowds by Jesus' ministry. For some time they had been working to discredit Jesus, and, if that did not work, to eliminate him. Each of these groups was conspiring to destroy the hopes and dreams of Jesus' followers. These outside forces were at work to crush his vision of reality.

A third reason that the two disciples on the road to Emmaus were wounded in their hopes and dreams is that they shared a faulty view of what the Messiah would look like and what he would do. The common expectation was for a military leader who would overthrow and drive out the Romans, restore David's throne, and bring peace and prosperity. Instead of a conquering hero who was strong in battle, they got a suffering servant who died on a cross.

We, too, can be wounded in hopes and dreams because of reversal of fortunes. When my father was a sophomore at Penn State University, his father died. Being the oldest child, he had to return home to help his mother raise his brothers and sister. His dream of a college degree was permanently put on hold.

Illness can also bring reversal of fortunes. Many families know the devastating impact of cancer and how it can disrupt and crush hopes and dreams. In the flash of a moment an accident can derail the best laid plans and create a new and difficult future.

While reversal of fortunes has a more localized context, being wounded because of outside forces has a much wider impact. A large segment of our population had to revise or adjust their hopes and dreams because of the decline of the stock market several years ago. Retirees found that their incomes were drastically cut and they were either going to have to adjust their lifestyles or look for additional sources of income. Every month their income was less and less and less. People in their fifties and sixties who were planning to retire early, saw their portfolios cut in half, which meant they had to reconsider their decisions.

Educational and charitable institutions for whom a significant amount of their income came from their investments, had to make radical adjustments. No longer were colleges and universities in a position to offer as many scholarships as they once had. Foundations found that their income from their investments was drastically reduced, which meant that there was less money to distribute. No longer did they have the funds to underwrite all of the programs they had previously supported. Outside forces can reverse our fortunes and affect our hope.

The third cause for the two on the road to Emmaus to be wounded was their unrealistic hopes and dreams. Not only can individuals be wounded because of unrealistic hopes and dreams, so can institutions. Lee was a rural church in White County, Indiana. With the exception of a handful of people, its membership was all over 65. One of their hopes and dreams was to attract young people so that the church might continue after they were gone. Sounds good. Unfortunately, the demographics of the township in which the church was located were identical to those of the church. There was hardly a child or youth to be found. In fact, there were very few people under the age of 55. Their hopes and dreams for their church were very unrealistic for their situation. They needed goals that focused around what they did well and which were relevant for their neighbors.

Another source of being wounded in our hopes and dreams that is hard to avoid is changing stages of life. Early in life, we establish hopes and dreams of things we would like to do, activities we would like to try, and the achievements we would like to accomplish. Usually, in our fifties, the reality of just how much we will be able to do, how many things we will have the opportunity to try, and the level of our accomplishments becomes clear. There is the realization that hopes and dreams we have had since we were in our teens or early twenties will never come to pass.

This reality check can result in a serious midlife crisis. The second highest incidences of divorce take place between the twentieth and the twenty-fifth years of marriage. In one final last attempt to hold on to one's youth with all of its dreams and expectations, there is one last grasp to act and behave like a teenager.

Perhaps by finding a younger partner the vitality of adolescence might last just a little longer.

Graduating from high school or college, marriage, the arrival of children, an empty nest, or retirement can also be the occasion for a person to be wounded in his or her hopes and dreams. Each of these normal changes can cause serious disruption.

Not only can we be wounded by changing stages of life, but by our inability to adjust to changes to our situation in general. The hopes and dreams we once had are no longer appropriate for new and different situations. When I was growing up, a profession that was in great demand and was guaranteed a good income if one was willing to work, was the television repairman. If the television would begin to act up, there was never a thought to buy a new one — they were too expensive. You called the local serviceman, hoped that he could work you into his schedule, and wait for him to make a house call. Sometimes he would be able to fix the set at the house, other times he would give you the dreaded bad news, "I will need to take it in." Today, when our televisions begin to act up, it is cheaper and quicker just to buy a new one, rather than have the old one repaired.

If a person is interested in electronics today, the field with great opportunity is not repairing televisions, but working on computers. There is a great demand for persons who can help people learn the basics of how to program and operate their computers. Even more in demand is someone who can be there when our computer crashes or, God forbid, when it becomes infected with a virus. Over these last fifty years, television repairmen who failed to change their hopes and dreams from a profession in electronics to computers or some of our other modern marvels, find that they have a lot of time on their hands.

Two other causes of our being wounded in our hopes and dreams is criticism from others, and repeated defeats. Both of these can wear one down to the point of just giving up. Rather than looking forward to the future with hope and expectation, the goal becomes to survive another week, another day, or perhaps just another hour. This can lead to a complete lack of hope for the future.

Even though Terkel had titled his book, *Hope Dies Last*, it can die. When it dies, the will to live grows dim.

When the risen Christ meets the two people on the road to Emmaus, what does he do? First, he walks with them, listening to their shattered dreams and expectations. He inquires concerning the source of their distress. Then and only then, does he begin to share with them the true nature and destiny of the Messiah, interpreting for them the scriptures about himself.

Here we have a process by which the risen Christ can take upon himself the place in our lives where we have been wounded in our hopes and dreams and bring new hopes and dreams. Jesus comes and walks with us, listening to our pain. Sometimes it is in the form of another person who becomes the instrument of his listening. At other times it is as one pours out the depths of his or her heart in prayer. Christ prods us with questions to help us clarify and sharpen our thinking. Slowly, Jesus begins to reveal to us the word we need to hear, to offer us a comforting embrace, to challenge us to move forward with confidence and strength. Out of the ashes of our broken hopes and dreams, he helps us create new hopes and dreams for the future.

This morning, Jesus would come and walk with us. He stands ready to listen where we are wounded in our hopes and our dreams. Let us pause to reflect where we may have experienced reversals of fortune or have had our hopes and dreams shattered because of outside forces. Perhaps our suffering is a result of unrealistic hopes and dreams. Change, both positive and negative, can be a source of being wounded. We may suffer as a result of going through the normal changes of life or because of our inability to adjust to our changed circumstances. Criticism from others or constant defeats can cause us to lose our hope for the future.

In this coming week, let us open our hearts and minds that Jesus might speak to us as he spoke to the two people on the road to Emmaus. May our hearts burn within us and may Jesus reveal to us his special word as we struggle with the places in our lives where we are wounded in our hopes and dreams.

Bulletin Insert

Fourth Sunday In Lent

Wounded In Our Relationships

Isaiah 52:13—53:3
James 4:1-10
Matthew 27:35-37

Sermon Notes

Causes
    Harmful relationships
    Loss of a significant person
    Loneliness
    Physical separation
    Emotional separation

Cure
> *Even though I walk through the darkest valley,*
> *I fear no evil;*
> *for you are with me;*
> *your rod and your staff —*
> *they comfort me.*
>
> — Psalm 23:4

Sermon

Wounded In Our Relationships
Isaiah 52:13—53:3; James 4:1-10; Matthew 27:35-37

> *Hands*
> *They can greet an old friend or inflict a severe blow.*
> *They can embrace a loved one or push away an unwanted advance.*
> *They can be lifted to heaven in praise or be wrung together in anguish.*
> *They can be extended in greeting or shook in anger.*
> *They can comfort a child or be the source of abuse.*
> *They can be instruments of healing or of destruction.*
> *They can be agents of good or of evil.*
> — Author unknown

Hands are the physical manifestation of the state of our relationships. They give expression to our thoughts, our emotions and our spirit, our hopes and our dreams. The first three wounds of Christ have focused on what is inside each of us, our inner self. The last two wounds will focus the self we show to others: our relationships and our actions. Most of the time what is inside us shapes how we interact with what is outside us. The places we are wounded on the inside can cause us to be wounded on the outside as well. In Matthew, Jesus tells the crowd, "But what comes out of the mouth proceeds from the heart, and this is what defiles. For out of the heart comes evil intentions, murder, adultery, fornication, theft, false witness, slander" (Matthew 15:18-19). Thus, this morning as we look at the places we may be wounded in our relationships, we need to keep in mind the places where we are wounded in our thoughts, in our emotions and spirit, in our hopes and dreams for they may be the source of our broken relations.

An obvious place we can be wounded in our relationships is when they are harmful or destructive. We can be wounded physically and/or emotionally if we are in an abusive relationship. Domestic violence in the United States occurs once every fifteen seconds. Annually, 4,000 women die as a result of spousal abuse.

Every year, nearly three million children are reported abused or neglected. That comes out to about two cases every minute. We can be wounded in our relationships if our friends are involved with drugs, drink alcohol in excess, or practice immoral behavior.

Our relationships can also be harmful if they are consistently negative. There are those people who, because of their attitudes, choice of words, critical nature, or general outlook on life, drain us emotionally and spiritually when we are around them for any length of time. You dread it when it is necessary to be in contact with such persons. They drain you of your energy, your joy, and your positive attitude about life. The easiest solution to such a problem would be to just avoid such people, but this is not realistic when they are close relatives, neighbors, or coworkers. Sometimes, there is no way you can avoid their negative influence.

A second place where we can become wounded in our relationships is because of the loss of a significant person in our life. The usual reason for this loss is death, but it can also be the result of a divorce, an illness that destroys the personality of someone that we have known for years, or an unexplained disappearance. This kind of wound is commonly identified as grief. Grieving is a normal part of the process of dealing with the death of a loved one or close friend. While all of us mourn differently, there are some generally accepted standards of what is appropriate and what is inappropriate. When our grief is normal, there comes the time when we can finally move on with our life.

When grief is inappropriate and long lasting, it can cause serious wounds. I was visiting the parents of a young man who had died under rather mysterious circumstances. His death appeared to be a suicide, but there was the lingering suspicion that he had been murdered by his wife. As we were talking, I noticed this urn on their mantle, accompanied by a picture of a small child. The vase contained the ashes of a grandchild who had been dead for a number of years. From my previous conversations with the couple, I had assumed that the grandchild was still alive. The couple had never come to terms with the fact that the child was dead. If they were stuck in their grieving for their grandchild, I was left to wonder how they would deal with the death of their son.

While we usually think of the loss of relationships having to do with people, it can sometimes have to do with pets or possessions. This is especially true if someone has an inappropriate attachment with an animal or a prized belonging. One night, I was awaked by a phone call for a distraught lady who asked if I would pray for her sick cat. On another occasion, I was asked if I would have a graveside service for a person's dog who had died.

A third area where we can be wounded in our relationships is loneliness. It's sometimes called, "alienation" or "estrangement." Just because we are experiencing loneliness does not necessarily mean that we are wounded in our relationships. Bruce Larson, in an article for the October, 1974, *Faith@Work* magazine, portrays loneliness as having the potential of being a positive force in our lives. For Larson, loneliness can be a precious gift when "it comes out of our deep humanity and forces us to deal with our original sin of willful separation from God, man and ourselves." It can be the occasion to get in touch with who we are and whose we are. It is when loneliness becomes a chronic condition that it wounds.

Many phone systems have a number that you can call to find out the current time and temperature. For most of us this is a source of information, but for the following person it was the only connection with a real person. "I have felt so intense a need to hear the sound of an adult human voice, especially during the lonely hours of the night, that I have dialed the time and just listened to it for a while. This helps at first, but then I feel shame for having to resort to such a thing."

A number of years ago in *Science Digest* (July, 1975), William A. Sadler, Jr., identified loneliness as the forgotten social problem. People suffering from chronic alienation may well live around and among us, but they never feel they're living with us. Sadler says, "The first and most outstanding feature of loneliness is a painful feeling, sometimes experienced as a sharp ache, as in moments of grief or separation; but it can also be a dull, lingering form of stress that seems to tear a person down." A feeling of alienation is a signal that something is missing in our lives. Loneliness has many causes: bad tapes that tell us "I'm not okay," a fear of love and relationships, or outside factors. In our high-tech, impersonal world, loneliness is a serious problem.

Starting with the war in Afghanistan and continuing with the conflict in Iraq, there are many families in our country who are experiencing being wounded in their relationships because of physical separation. Parents worry about their sons or daughters serving in harm's way. Spouses are left to raise children by themselves while their partners are gone for a year or more. Husband and wife are separated because one is assigned to serve in one country while the other is assigned to a different country. Emails and occasional phone calls make the separation somewhat more bearable, but there is the constant worry concerning how it is going and what dangers the loved one faces.

Some would say that we suffer being wounded in our relationships because of the loss of the close intergenerational family. When I was growing up, my family lived first in Cortland, Ohio, and then in Gary, Indiana. Most of my cousins lived in Beaver, Pennsylvania, with the rest just an hour away. Maybe once or twice a year I would have the opportunity of being with them, and then only for a short time. Over the years, I grew to resent the fact that my family lived in Ohio and then Indiana, preventing me from being with my cousins on a regular basis. The only real advantage I had over any of them was that my maternal grandmother lived with us the last ten years of her life. However, even this advantage had its downsides.

One source of grief that was not mentioned earlier, is the empty nest. A couple spends twenty to 25 years raising their children, buying a house that will accommodate their brood, then wake up one day, finding that they are rattling around a big place all by themselves. The wounds of the physical separation of children can lead into our final sources of being wounded in our relationships: emotional separation. With the kids gone, a couple can wake up one morning and discover that they no longer know each other. Over the years their lives have gone separate ways. For a long time each have been each doing their own thing. The love that was once there is now gone.

The opposite of love is not hate, but indifference. Emotional separation can creep into our relationships through the simple process of gradually caring less and less about another person. It finally comes to the point of simply being indifferent to what is happening in his or her life. With the children gone, a couple can discover that they have become strangers sleeping in the same bed. The only connection they had, the children, is now gone.

Another cause of emotional separation is anger. As we have already noted, extreme anger can be the cause of us being wounded in our relationships when it takes the form of abuse. It can also be the source of us being wounded when it is not resolved properly. Most of us have been trained to deal with anger by either avoiding it, capitulating to it, seeking a compromise, or letting it have its way. Jim Campbell, who works in the area of labor relations, says that in dealing with conflict all we do is set ourselves up for the next conflict. Today's compromise just sets us up for tomorrow's conflict.

Sometimes we are wounded in our relationships because of the places we are wounded in our emotions and spirit. This is especially true for anger. If we have not learned how to manage the emotion of anger in our lives, then it is sure to cause serious disruptions in our relationships. In one of the churches that I served was a lady, Marge, who was rightfully angry with her birth mother who was an alcoholic that physically and emotionally abused her. When she was quite young, Marge's father divorced her mother and married another woman who was the exact opposite of her biological mother. She offered the young girl the love and care she had never known to this point in her life.

Unfortunately, rather than accepting the love of her new stepmother, Marge continued to hoard her anger and resentment toward her natural mother. Not only did she hate her mother, she also hated her father for allowing the abuse, and she hated society in general for not doing anything to rescue her. Over the years, her anger had gradually grown and grown, finally destroying her relationships with her father, her husband, and her three children. Marge's goal became to get back at the world by having them take care of her. Tragically, she got her wish, for Marge ended her life in the back ward of a nursing home, isolated and alone.

During this Lenten and Easter season, we proclaim that Jesus died on the cross to set us free from the bonds of sin and death. He was wounded to set us free from the places we are wounded. Jesus was wounded on his hands to set us free from the places in our lives where we are wounded because of harmful relationships or emotional separation. Both of these have allowed sin to enter into our lives. Our destructive relationships and emotions hold us in bondage. We find ourselves unable to escape their grip. By accepting the gift of Christ's death on the cross and his offer of forgiveness and new life, these shackles can be broken.

When we are wounded in our relationships, Jesus offers us a healthy relationship. Because of the resurrection, he breaks the bondage of the wounds that prevent us from being in relationship. He sets us free first to love ourselves and then to love others. The way he does this is by entering into relationship with us. As we know his love and grace, we have the places where we are wounded in our relationship healed.

Jesus is sometimes described as the Good Shepherd who is willing to lay down his life for his sheep. When we walk through the dark valleys of harmful relationships, death and grief, loneliness, physical separation, and emotional separation, we have the assurance that Jesus is with us. He will offer his rod and his staff to comfort us and give us the assurance of his presence. Then once we have been reconciled to Jesus, he will help us to be reconciled to ourselves and to our neighbors.

Pause for a few moments to take inventory of the places that we are wounded in our relationships because of harmful relationships, because of the loss of a significant person or possibly an object, because of loneliness, because of physical separation, or perhaps emotional separation. Then let us turn to Jesus that he might come to us this morning and offer us the opportunity to be in relationship with him. Let us each open ourselves to the eternal love that God offers to us as a result of his Son's death on a cross. Then the miracle can take place. We can love others because God, through his Son, first loved us.

Bulletin Insert

Fifth Sunday In Lent

Wounded In Our Actions

Isaiah 53:4-9
James 1:22-25
John 19:16-18

Sermon Notes

Causes
- Accidents
  - Automobile
  - Household
  - Recreation
- Bad luck
  - Wrong place at the wrong time
- Bad decisions
  - Finances
  - Purchases
  - Business
- Impulsive acts
  - Get caught up in the moment
  - Impulsive buying
  - Impulsive actions

Cure

[Peter said] "Lord, Save me!" Jesus immediately reached out his hand and caught him, saying to him, "You of little faith, why did you doubt?" — Matthew 14:30d, 31

Sermon

Wounded In Our Actions
Isaiah 53:4-9; James 1:22-25; John 19:16-18

At New Smyrna Beach, an elderly man approached the water's edge and started to wade in. Watching him were two teenagers who noticed that he was wearing an expensive-looking watch. Thinking that it might not be waterproof, one of them called out to warn him. The gentleman thanked them for the warning, took off his watch, put it in a small pocket in his swimming trunks, and continued into the surf.

A harried wife, after spending much time at her desk, announced to her husband and children: "Well, I worked out a budget. But one of us will have to go."

Last week we considered possible places where we may be wounded in our relationships, this week we will examine areas where we may be injured because of our actions. Our opening vignettes suggest three such possibilities: being wounded because of accidents, because of bad decisions, and because of impulsive acts. This morning, in addition to these three, we will be considering a fourth source of being wounded: bad luck. Just as having difficulties with our relationships may be an outgrowth of being wounded in our thoughts, our emotions and spirit, our hopes and dreams, these may also be possible causes of a person being wounded in their actions. This is especially true if the reason for the injury is either a bad decision or an impulsive act.

A motorist is driving down a busy highway. A front tire blows, causing the driver to lose control. The car swerves across the median, hitting an oncoming car, killing its driver and two of the three passengers. The driver of the first car is hospitalized for many months, incurs medical bills that exceed the limits of his insurance, is sued by the families of the people in the other car, and finds he is haunted with being the cause of the deaths of three people. Almost every day our papers have at least one incident of people being wounded because of an automobile accident.

Statistics indicate that the most common place for accidents is the home. This is particularly true of the bathroom. A wet floor, a loose rug, or a missed step can result in broken bones, a severe cut, or a serious head injury. A person living alone may not be found for several days, causing additional problems because of dehydration. A lady in one of my former churches fell in the bathroom, was unable to get up, and was not found for three days. By then it was too late. She died a few days later as a result of being seriously deficient in body fluids. Because of their adventuresome spirit, children are especially susceptible to household accidents.

When I was a junior in high school, the star of the high school basketball team was killed in a hunting accident. While climbing a fence, he accidentally dropped his shotgun that then discharged, killing him instantly. The entire school was closed the day of his funeral and my sophomore class was taken by bus to the funeral home for his viewing. Recreation is meant to bring about re-creation and enjoyment, but it can also be a major source of accidents that may bring about us being wounded in our actions.

An old comical expression goes: "If it weren't for bad luck, I would have no luck at all." We can be wounded in our actions simply because of bad luck. We just happen to be at the wrong place at the wrong time. The outcome of much of what happens in life is based on statistical probabilities. If you have ever had a surgical procedure, you would have been asked to sign a consent form. Have you ever read these forms completely through? It will scare you to death. The form indicates the possible complications that might arise by having the procedure. The problem can be anywhere from something very minor to death itself. It is only after you are near the end that you learn that the statistical probability of any of these complications occurring is very small, but having said this, there is always the chance that you might have the bad luck of being the one time in a thousand that something goes wrong.

When I was working as a volunteer chaplain of the day for a hospital in northeast Indiana, a child having a tonsillectomy never woke up. No reason was ever discovered for the tragedy. Several months before, he had surgery that involved being completely anesthetized, and he had come through fine. A sense of melancholy hung over the hospital for months. This was unfortunately the one person in a thousand for whom the anesthesia did not work as it should.

A third place that we can be wounded in our actions is by making bad decisions. A few years after I left a church where I had been the associate for two years, they made a major addition to their facilities. What they did not realize was that their funding package involved a rather substantial final balloon clause. When the payment came due, they were forced to eliminate the associate pastor position, radically cut back on their general expenses, and still look for ways to raise additional funds. The bad decision made in securing funding for the new addition caused the church to be wounded in their programming and outreach for a number of years.

We can be wounded in our actions by making a bad decision in a purchase. A number of years ago, I had this impulse to buy a chipper/mulcher. We had a lot of trees on the parsonage property and I had convinced myself that I could save a huge amount of money by making my own mulch. Would any of you like a good deal on a chipper/mulcher? Do any of you have this impulse that you just can't do without one? Since I have owned the rather expensive machine, I would guess that I have not made more than ten bags of mulch. That comes to about $20 per bag.

There is a commercial on television in which a couple has bought the home of their dreams. Unfortunately the contractor that they have hired tells them the foundation is bad, the roof needs to be replaced, the wiring has to be updated, and the house has termites. Their dream home has very quickly become a money trap that will bleed them dry.

Poor business decisions can also be a source of being injured because of our actions. In our volatile and ever-changing world, it is not always easy to determine where a business should invest its resources for the future. As we saw earlier with the example of the television repairman, what is a lucrative and in-demand business today, may be nonexistent in ten or fifteen years. Sometimes poor business decisions are made on the basis of bad information. Other times they occur because of a lack of experience, and then there are the times they do not turn out for the best simply because of bad luck.

A possible cause of making bad decisions with finances, a purchase, or in business is being impulsive. I remember when I was in college an insurance salesman came by my dorm room selling this great deal on whole life policies. Despite the fact that my father had already purchased a policy for me and I did not have any financial obligations other than possible funeral expenses, I got caught up in the moment and bought a policy. The policy was not needed, far too expensive, and became a real drain on my financial resources. It took me several years to extricate myself from a simple impulsive act one evening in a dorm room.

Usually when our actions are well thought out and reasoned they do not cause us problems. It is when they are made impulsively that they can have serious consequences. Accidents and bad decisions may occur because of impetuous or spur-of-the-moment action. Most of us are not very good at making snap decisions.

In the New Testament, the quintessential example of a person who gets himself into trouble because of impulsive words and actions is the Apostle Peter. Matthew tells the story of when the disciples were traveling from the east side of the Sea of Galilee to the west. Jesus had remained behind to pray. As can happen very quickly, a storm comes up causing the disciples to be greatly distressed. Jesus sees their plight and comes to them, walking on the waters of the Sea of Galilee. When Peter sees his Lord, he tells him, "Lord, if it is your wish, command me to come to you on the water." Jesus answers, "Come." Impulsively, Peter gets out of the boat and begins to walk toward Jesus. He does fine until he becomes distracted by the strong winds and starts to sink. He cries out to Jesus, "Save me!" Immediately, Jesus reaches out his hand and catches the impulsive disciple.

When Peter realizes that he is in serious trouble as a result of his impetuous action of getting out of the boat, he very quickly asks Jesus for help. Would that each of us might do the same when we are wounded in our actions because of an impulsive act, an accident, a bad decision, or simply bad luck. Would that we might call out for Jesus to come and save us, for him to reach his hand out to us and pull us out of the deep.

The chances of our being wounded in our actions in the future are high. Because of an impulsive act, an accident, a bad decision, or simply bad luck, we may well find ourselves sinking under the weight of a heavy burden. At such times we have the assurance that if we call, Jesus will come. He will be there to reach out his hand and help to bring about healing and wholeness.

Let us now pause to examine our lives to see where we are wounded because of an accident, bad luck, bad decision, or an impulsive act. As we find ourselves sinking under the weight of our actions, let us reach out our hands to Jesus that he might come and pull us out of the deep. As we reflect on the past, this may also be a time for us to ask Jesus to be with us in the future to prevent us from making impulsive decisions and actions that will only get us into trouble.

Palm Sunday
(The Sixth Sunday In Lent)

Several times in the book of Revelation there is a break in the action here on earth while we are transported to heaven. This is especially true when the action has gotten particularly intense and one feels in need of some relief and, more importantly, a word of assurance. For me, during the Lenten season, Palm Sunday has always provided a similar break in the action. It offers a much needed respite before the final push to Good Friday.

Recently there has been a trend to expand Palm Sunday to include the events of the passion. I suspect that one of the reasons for this change is the poor attendance at Maundy Thursday and Good Friday services. For the majority of a worshiping congregation, if they do not hear the story of passion on Palm Sunday they will not hear it at all. *Wounded For Us* is designed to encourage people to attend the church's observances of Maundy Thursday and Good Friday. Thus, the services for the Sunday before Easter have as their primary focus just Palm Sunday. However, one of them does include the events of Monday, Tuesday, and Wednesday of Holy Week.

Service One was used in conjunction with the service for the first five Sundays in Lent. As a part of the service a sixth and final Lenten purple candle is extinguished. Churches will want to adapt the service to incorporate their normal Palm Sunday traditions. The Call To Worship is the same as the one used for the first five Sundays in Lent. The Prayer of Consecration following the offertory is taken from *A Time For Worship* by John Enochs (CSS Publishing Co., Lima, Ohio, 1991, p. 64). While it is not included in this suggested service, an adaptation of "Were You There?" such as "Were you there when he rode into Jerusalem?" might be used for the extinguishing of a sixth Lenten candle.

Service Two liturgically retells the story of Holy Week from Palm Sunday through Wednesday. The service follows the events of Jesus' last week using the Gospel of Matthew. The story could also be told using one of the other gospels or perhaps even a combination of them.

There are two options for the extinguishing of Lenten candles. Option 1 is similar to the first service in that just one candle is used. Option 2 involves the use of four candles, one each for Palm Sunday, Monday, Tuesday, and Wednesday. Churches using Option 2 may also want to have an additional candle for Maundy Thursday.

The service ends with words: "To Be Continued." It is a way to remind the worshipers that the story of Holy Week will be continuing the following Thursday when the church will be fulfilling Jesus' command to remember the events of the Upper Room.

Following Service One is a sermon that identifies a sixth Lenten candle for the places where we are wounded as a society. More specifically, it centers on the places that Jerusalem was wounded when Jesus rode into the city on the first Palm Sunday. As with the sermons for the first five Sundays in Lent, it begins with "Sermon Notes."

After Service Two are two of the suggested scripture readings used in the service: Matthew 21:18—22:14 (Selected) and Matthew 24:1—25:46 (Selected). When the second service was used at Crescent Avenue United Methodist Church in Fort Wayne, Indiana, the two parables were read from a translation by Clarence Jordan.

Service One
Worship Service

Palm Sunday

Prelude

Call To Worship   Hebrews 4:14-16
Since, then, we have a great high priest who has passed through the heavens, Jesus, the Son of God,
let us hold fast to our confession.
For we do not have a high priest who is unable to sympathize with our weaknesses,
but we have one who in every respect has been tested as we are, yet without sin.
Let us therefore approach the throne of grace with boldness,
so that we may receive mercy and find grace to help in time of need.

Hymn Of Gathering   "Hosanna, Loud Hosanna"

Collect

Announcements

Morning Prayers

The Lord's Prayer

Anthem

Scripture Reading   Matthew 21:1-11
    Jesus Enters Jerusalem

Offering Of Ourselves, Our Commitments, And Our Gifts
Offertory Sentence
Then he said to them, "Give therefore to the emperor the things that are the emperor's, and to God the things that are God's" (Matthew 22:21b, c).

Offertory

Prayer of Consecration
Lord of life, our world asks so much from us. In this moment of giving remind us that our offerings reach out to heal and make new the world beyond our doors. Amen.

Hymn Of Preparation "O God Of Every Nation"

Sermon "A City In Turmoil"

Extinguish Sixth Lenten Candle *(Option 1)*

Hymn Of Going "Where Cross The Crowded Ways Of Life"

Sending Forth

Congregational Benediction "Near The Cross" (vv. 1, 3)
Jesus, keep me near the cross; there a precious fountain, free to all, a healing stream, flows from Calvary's mountain. In the cross, in the cross, be my glory ever, till my raptured soul shall find rest beyond the river.
Near the cross! O Lamb of God, bring its scenes before me, help me walk from day to day with its shadows o'er me. In the cross, in the cross, be my glory ever, till my raptured soul shall find rest beyond the river.

Postlude

To Be Continued ...

Bulletin Insert

Palm Sunday

A City In Turmoil

Matthew 21:1-11

Sermon Notes
Jesus' Lament Over Jerusalem

Jerusalem, Jerusalem, the city that kills the prophets and stones those who are sent to it! How often have I desired to gather your children together as a hen gathers her brood under her wings, and you were not willing! See, your house is left to you, desolate. For I tell you, you will not see me again until you say, "Blessed is the one who comes in the name of the Lord."
— Matthew 23:37-39

Jerusalem: A Wounded City
  Politically
  Religiously
  Socially
  Economically

Cure

Then I saw a new heaven and a new earth; for the first heaven and the first earth had passed away, and the sea was no more. And I saw the holy city, the new Jerusalem, coming down out of heaven from God, prepared as a bride adorned for her husband.
— Revelation 21:1, 2

Sermon

A City In Turmoil
Matthew 21:1-11

The Gospel of Matthew's rendering of Jesus' triumphant entry on Palm Sunday describes Jerusalem as being *in turmoil*. Everyone wanted to know, who was this person riding on a colt? Was Jesus the long-expected Messiah? Was he a revolutionary leader who might cause riots in the streets? Was he a threat to the power of Rome? Was he a religious leader who would challenge the religious establishment? No wonder Jerusalem found itself in turmoil.

The Jerusalem into which Jesus rode was also a wounded city. It was wounded politically, religiously, economically, and socially. *(Note: the one giving this message may want to identify how Jerusalem was wounded, using additional or different categories.)* The arrival of Jesus poured salt into the places where it was hurting and afflicted.

First, Jerusalem was wounded politically. Herod Antipas, son of Herod the Great, was the tetrarch of Galilee and Perea. Like his father, he was a builder, founding the present-day city of Tiberias. Because John the Baptist had called into question the appropriateness of his marriage to Herodias, Herod had John the Baptist put to death. It was no accident that Herod was called by Jesus "that fox." Until he was deposed in 39/40 A.D., "that fox" ruled with craftiness and cunning.

On Palm Sunday, Herod Antipas was in town for the Passover. The people knew that he was well aware of Jesus and his ministry. Several times the tetrarch had indicated that he would like to talk with this worker of wonders and miracles. There was a general consensus that Herod found Jesus to be a threat to his power and position. And the people knew, from the beheading of John, what happens to those who threaten Herod.

Pontius Pilate, the procurator of Judea, was also in Jerusalem for the Passover. His normal residence was in Caesarea, but Jewish holidays found him in the Holy City because of the potential for riots. The turmoil caused by the entrance of Jesus on a colt on

Palm Sunday gave him great cause for concern. This was not the first time that he was faced with potential problems on a Jewish religious holiday. Pilate's inability to deal with such incidents would eventually cause his removal.

When Pilate was in town, it would seem likely that he would set up shop at the Antonia Fortress. Its tower provided an excellent vantage point to monitor what was happening on the temple mount. As Jesus rode down the Mount of Olives, the soldiers who were billeted at the fortress were able to observe the whole incident. One can only wonder what was going through their minds. Would they be called upon to put down another riot?

Second, Jerusalem was also wounded religiously. Jesus made it clear in his teaching that most of those in religious authority put heavy burdens on the people rather than giving them relief from their burdensome loads. He says to the teachers of the Jewish law, "Woe also to your lawyers! For you load people with burdens hard to bear, and you yourselves do not lift a finger to ease them" (Luke 11:46). In their conduct of the temple, the priests took advantage of the people, finding all sorts of schemes to extract additional revenues from them.

While the different religious groups were unified in their burdening the people, they were far from united in their religious beliefs and practices. There were strong and at times violent differences between the Pharisees, the Sadducees, the priests, the Essenes, and the Zealots. Even within groups there were differences that tended to cause deep divisions. The Pharisees contained at least two groups: the more conservative followers of the House of Shammai and the more liberal adherents of the House of Hillel. There is some indication that Jesus may have belonged to this former group.

Third, Jerusalem was wounded economically. Jesus has been described as coming for the least, the last, and the lost. With some notable exception, those who were a part of the crowds that came to see and hear him, fit this description. Many of those who lined the way the first Palm Sunday who were his followers came from this segment of the population. On the other side of the temple mount lived the very rich. One of the sources for their wealth was to exploit the least, the last, and the lost. On Palm Sunday, with the arrival of Jesus, these two groups clash as they come into contact with each other.

Finally, Jerusalem was wounded socially. In many ways this is a consequence of being wounded politically, religiously, and economically. Jerusalem was divided into many competing social groups. On the one hand there were the righteous Pharisees and on the other the sinners and tax collectors. As we have seen there were the divisions due to the various religious parties. The influential, the important, and the powerful was contrasted with the least, the last, and the lost.

Today our newspapers, radios, and televisions remind us that Jerusalem remains a wounded city. The three religious groups for whom it is a holy city — Christians, Jews, and Muslims — seem to be in a perpetual state of conflict. Even Christian groups find it hard to coexist. On my first visit to the Church of the Holy Sepulchre just north of the traditional burial place of Jesus was a huge scaffolding that I learned had been there for some time. It would seem that the four groups in charge of the church — Greek Orthodox, Romans Catholics, Armenians, and Copts — had been unable to agree on what needed to be done, so nothing was done. On another visit our tour group had to leave the temple square because fundamental Orthodox Jews were congregating in preparation for their protesting at the Israeli Knesset.

(The purpose of the next section of this sermon is to articulate how a particular congregation is located in a wounded environment. Each pastor will want to tailor this segment to conform to the specific concerns facing the people.)

The book of Revelation tells us that Jerusalem will ultimately be healed with the coming of the new age. "Then I saw a new heaven and a new earth; for the first heaven and the first earth had passed away, and the sea was no more. And I saw the holy city, the new Jerusalem, coming down out of heaven from God, prepared as a bride adorned for her husband" (Revelation 21:1, 2). Until the return of Jesus we live in the in-between. Today we only catch glimpses of what it will be like when the new Jerusalem comes and all people live in peace and harmony together, when there is no more sickness or disease.

A common image of the coming kingdom of God is the great banquet. Today we have a foretaste of this feast when we gather to celebrate the Lord's Supper. When Jesus gathered with his disciples in the Upper Room, he told them that he would not eat with them again until that time that he would be with them at the heavenly banquet. The broken bread symbolizes the places in our lives where we are wounded. The wine represents the power of God to heal our wounds both in the here and now and ultimately by resurrection and the coming of the New Jerusalem.

In the Lord's Supper we receive a glimpse of the coming kingdom of God. This vision should encourage and empower us to engage our wounded world, but it should also help to sensitize us to look for those places in our normal everyday activities where this coming kingdom is also breaking in.

(At this point the pastor may want to also connect this glimpse of the coming kingdom of God with the places identified as to where the congregation finds themselves in a wounded world.)

Not only are we personally wounded, we also find ourselves living in a world that is wounded politically, religiously, socially, and economically. We wait in eager anticipation for the coming of the New Jerusalem. In the in-between let us look for signs of this in-breaking of the kingdom of God. As the places in our lives where we are wounded become healed, we have a taste of the true nature of what it means when the rule of God shall come; they are precursor of the arrival of the New Jerusalem.

**Service Two
Worship Service**

Palm/Passion Sunday

Prelude

The First Palm Sunday
Palm Sunday Scripture Reading   Matthew 21:1-11
    Triumphal Entry

Call To Worship
    This is the day to let your heart take control of your lips.
    We can't keep silent. Our hearts are bursting with praise for Jesus, king of our lives.
    In spite of the shadow of the cross over the palm-strewn way, Jesus rules in the hearts of those who surrender to him.
    We commit ourselves wholly to Jesus, and ask him to have his way with us.

Hymn   "All Glory, Laud, And Honor"

Collect
    O Lord God, whose Son followed your will, both as a servant and as Savior, and now rules in the hearts of those who accept him as king; open our hearts to his rule; that we may rejoice in the blessings of his kingdom, and share with those who honor him with their lives. In his name we pray. Amen.

Anthem

Scripture Reading   Matthew 21:12-17
    Jesus Goes To The Temple

Pastoral Prayer

The Lord's Prayer

Extinguish A Lenten Candle *(Option 2)*

Monday Of Holy Week

Invitation To Dance   "Lord Of The Dance"

Scripture Reading   Matthew 21:18—22:14
Rejection Of Jesus By Israel   *(Selected and paraphrased)*

Anthem

Scripture Reading   Matthew 22:15-22
Questions About Paying Taxes

Offering
Offertory

Offertory Sentence
Think of us in this way, as servants of Christ and stewards of God's mysteries. Moreover, it is required of stewards that they be found trustworthy (1 Corinthians 4:1, 2).

Doxology

Prayer Of Consecration
Lord of life, our world asks so much from us. In this moment of giving remind us that our offerings reach out to heal and make new the world beyond our doors. Amen.

Extinguish A Lenten Candle *(Option 2)*

Tuesday Of Holy Week

Scripture Reading   Matthew 24:1—25:46
The Coming Judgment   *(Selected and paraphrased)*

Hymn   "Soon And Very Soon"

Extinguish A Lenten Candle *(Option 2)*

Wednesday Of Holy Week
Scripture Reading   Matthew 26:1-5
   The Plot Against Jesus

Collect
   O Lord, whose victory in Jerusalem culminated in agony on Golgotha, deliver us from the temptation to turn your real passion into a pious parade. Remind us that your destination on that first Palm Sunday was not a festive coronation in the holy city but a final confirmation from God, that you spurned the offer of a royal crown to shoulder the shame of a criminal's cross; that you were able to save others only because you did not seek to save yourself. For us as for you, the cost of divine approval demands the devotion of our will to God. Amen.

Scripture Reading   Matthew 26:6-16
   Jesus Anointed At Bethany

Extinguish A Lenten Candle *(Options 1 and 2)*

Hymn Of Assurance   "He Touched Me"

Postlude

To Be Continued ...

Service Two
Selected Scripture Readings

Palm/Passion Sunday

Rejection Of Christ By Israel Matthew 21:18—22:14
(Selected and paraphrased)

Reader One: The first thing that Jesus did after entering Jerusalem was to go to the temple where he drove out the moneychangers. This act outraged the religious and Jewish authorities and the die was cast for the events that were to come.

When Jesus returned to Jerusalem after spending the night in the city of Bethany, the city was full of excitement about the events of the previous day. No sooner had Jesus returned to the temple than he was questioned about his authority.

Reader Two: The chief priests and the elders came to him and asked, "What right do you have to do these things? Who gave you such right?" Jesus answered them, "I will ask you just one question, and if you give me an answer, I will tell you what right I have to do these things. Where did John's right to baptize come from: was it from God or from man?" His opponents started to argue among themselves, "What shall we say? If we answer, 'From God,' he will say to us, 'Why, then, did you not believe John?' But if we say, 'From man,' we are afraid of what the people might do, because they are all convinced that John was a prophet." So they answered Jesus, "We don't know." And he said to them, "Neither will I tell you, then, by what right I do these things."

Reader One: Then Jesus tells three parables: the parable of the two sons, the parable of the tenants in the vineyard, and the parable of the wedding feast. These three stories make the same essential point: the chosen people of Israel have rejected God's own. Jesus accuses them of making a pretense of faith. They talk a good game, but they never put their faith into action.

Reader Two: There was a landowner who planted a vineyard, put a fence around it, dug a wine press in it, and built a watchtower. Then he leased it to tenants and went to another country. When the harvest time had come, he sent his slaves to the tenants to collect his produce. But the tenants seized his slaves and beat one, killed another, and stoned another. Again he sent other slaves, more than the first; and they treated them in the same way. Finally he sent his son to them, saying, "They will respect my son." But when the tenants saw the son, they said to themselves, "This is the heir; come; let us kill him and get his inheritance." So they seized him, threw him out of the vineyard, and killed him. Now when the owner of the vineyard comes, what will he do to those tenants? They said to him, "He will put those wretches to a miserable death, and lease the vineyard to other tenant who will give him the produce at the harvest time."

Jesus said to them, "Have you never read in the scriptures: 'The stone that the builders rejected has become the cornerstone; this was the Lord's doing, and it is amazing in our eyes'? Therefore I tell you, the kingdom of God will be taken away from you and given to a people that produces the fruits of the kingdom. The one who falls on this stone will be broken to pieces; and it will crush anyone on whom it falls" (Matthew 21:33-43).

The Coming Judgment Matthew 24:1—25:46
(Selected and paraphrased)

Reader One: In Matthew, the focus of Jesus' last Tuesday was on the coming judgment. Here we find the fifth and final teaching discourse in Matthew. Most of the activities of Holy Week take place in or around the temple. The destruction of the temple is to be a sign of the coming judgment.

Reader Two: Jesus left the temple when his disciples came to him to call his attention to its buildings. "Yes," he said, "you may well look at all these. I tell you this; not a single stone here will be left in its place; every one of them will be thrown down."

Reader One: Then Jesus goes on to describe the coming troubles and persecutions and what this awful horror will be like.

Reader Two: "Soon after the trouble of those days," Jesus continues, "The sun will grow dark, the moon will no longer shine, the stars will fall from heaven, and the powers in space will be driven from their courses. Then the sign of the Son of Man will appear in the sky; and all the peoples of the earth will weep as they see the Son of Man coming on the clouds of heaven with power and great glory. The great trumpet will sound, and he will send out his angels to the four corners of the earth, and they will gather his chosen people from one end of the world to the other."

Reader One: Then Jesus tells a series of stories and parables. The first three are concerned with the need to be watchful, for no one knows the time or place when Christ shall return. Therefore, at every moment of our lives we need to be ready.

Reader Two: For it is as if a man, going on a journey, summoned his slaves and entrusted his property to them; to one he gave five talents, to another two, to another one, to each according to his ability. Then he went away (Matthew 25:14-15).

Reader One: The one who had received the five talents went off at once and traded with them, and made five more talents. In the same way, the one who had the two talents made two more talents. But the one who had received the one talent went off and dug a hole in the ground and hid his master's money (Matthew 25:16-18).

Reader Two: After a long time the master of those slaves came and settled accounts with them. Then the one who had received the five talents, came forward, bringing five more talents, saying "Master, you have handed over to me five talents; see, I have made five more talents." His master said to him, "Well done, good and trustworthy slave; you have been trustworthy in a few things, I will put you in charge of many things; enter into the joy of your master" (Matthew 25:19-21).

Reader One: And the one with the two talents also came forward, saying, "Master, you handed over to me two talents; see, I have made two more talents." His master said to him, "Well done, good and trustworthy slave, you have been trustworthy in a few things, I will put you in charge of many things; enter into the joy of your master" (Matthew 25:22-23).

Reader Two: Then the one who had received the one talent also came forward, saying, "Master, I knew that you were a harsh man, gathering where you did not scatter seed; so I was afraid, and I went and hid your talent in the ground. Here you have what is yours." But his master replied, "You wicked and lazy slave! You knew, did you, that I reap where I did not sow, and gather where I did not scatter? Then you ought to have invested my money with the bankers, and on my return I would have received what was my own with interest. So take the talent from him, and give it to the one with the ten talents" (Matthew 25:24-28).

Reader One: For to all those who have, more will be given, and they will have an abundance; but from those who have nothing, even what they have will be taken away (Matthew 25:29).

Reader Two: As for this worthless slave, throw him into the outer darkness, where there will be weeping and gnashing of teeth (Matthew 25:30).

Maundy Thursday

As a child the first time I heard the word "maundy" I associated it with being seedy. It was only when I got to seminary that I learned that it meant "command." The Thursday evening of Holy Week, churches celebrate Holy Communion to fulfill our Lord's command to "do this in remembrance of me." Included for this emphasis of the five wounds of Christ is a Maundy Thursday worship service, with communion following a common meal.

The Maundy Thursday service was originally used at the Crescent Avenue United Methodist Church as a continuation of the second Palm Sunday service to be found earlier. Following the Gospel of Matthew, it traces the events of Thursday of Holy Week.

It was the tradition of Crescent Avenue to observe Maundy Thursday in the church's fellowship hall. At one end of the hall tables were set for a common meal. At the other end was a long table that had a large chair in the center with six chairs on either side. At either ends of the table were candelabras. The five votive candles used during the first five Sundays of Lent were placed in front of the large chair.

The service begins with the reading of Matthew 26:17-19, "Preparations For The Last Supper," followed by the lighting of the Lenten candles. The number of candles will depend upon how many candles the church decides to use as a part of its Lenten observance. In this service, the candles are not extinguished. The opening statement comes from the Jewish Passover. The prayer provides an introduction to the evening as well as serving as a prayer for the common meal that is to follow. An attempt was made to keep this meal in the fashion of a Jewish family Passover meal.

The service continues after the meal with the reading of Matthew 26:20-25, 31-38, "Prediction Of Judas' Betrayal And Peter's Denial," with a period of confession following. At this point a short homily may be included in which the people are invited to name the places in their lives that they have identified during the first six Sundays of Lent where they are broken. Next, Matthew 26:26-30 that tells of the institution of the Lord's Supper is read. The scripture reading is followed by the Prayer Of Great Thanksgiving.

The people are now invited to come in groups of twelve to partake of the Lord's Supper. In front of the large table is a basket of either large rolls or small loaves of bread. One roll/loaf is used with each table group. As the person presiding breaks one of the rolls/loaves he or she says, "The body of Christ broken from the places you are broken in your life." The person presiding then takes one of the halves and offers it to the person sitting at one end of the table with the words, "The body of Christ broken for you." The person takes a piece and then partakes. The bread is then handed to the next person who offers it to the person sitting next to him or her. In this way it is passed down the table.

For the service at Crescent Avenue a communion tray filled with plastic cups was used for the distribution of the juice. Before the distribution of the cups, the person in charge lifts one of them and says, "The blood of Christ, shed for you to bring about healing, new life, and resurrection." The juice is then distributed in a manner similar to the distribution of the bread. For both the bread and the juice, the person presiding may take a seat at the opposite end of the last table from where he or she started the two elements. In this way he or she may be served in the same manner as all of those attending the service.

While communion is being served, those remaining at the tables may want to join together in the singing of communion hymns or hymns appropriate for the occasion. At Crescent Avenue some of the hymns were sung by the choir, others by everyone. A song sheet was provided for the congregational hymns. Two or three members of the choir were a part of each table setting until the whole choir had been served. This ensured that there were always enough singers for each of the hymns.

The service ends with the reading of Matthew 26:30, 36-46, "Mount Of Olives And The Garden Of Gethsemane," followed by a prayer. Those attending the service are invited to return the following day for the church's observance of Good Friday. This invitation is offered with the words, "To Be Continued ..."

During the Lenten season, the Crescent Avenue United Methodist Church traditionally has a communion service on Wednesdays. The scripture reading was the Gospel Lesson from the previous Sunday. After the Lord's Prayer the communion bread is broken. Here the officiant may want to use the words: "The body of Christ broken for the places in *our* lives where *we* are broken (name the wound for the week)." For those churches that have communion weekly, they may want to adapt a form of this service for their use.

Worship Service

Maundy Thursday

Common Meal/Communion Service
Scripture Reading　　　　　　　　　　Matthew 26:17-19
　　Preparations For The Last Supper

Lighting Of The Candles
　　Praise to you God, Creator of the universe. You placed the sun, the moon, and the stars in the heavens. You warm our world and bring us springtime. You bring us this service of bread and wine. You bring us to this night of freedom.
　　Blessed are you, Creator of the universe, God of light and warmth.

Prayer
　　Blessed are you, eternal God, ruler of the universe, for the vine, precious, good, and spacious land that you gave to our ancestors, to eat of its fruit, and to enjoy its goodness. This night, we call to our memory that evening that your Son shared with his disciples a meal in the upper room. As he graced their gathering then may he grace our gathering tonight as we come in response to his command to do this in memory of him. As we gather around these tables, we ask that you would bless this bounty of our blessed nation that we might be mindful of the people who go to bed hungry each night. Amen.

Sharing Of The Meal

The Lord's Supper
Scripture Reading　　　　　　　　Matthew 26:20-25, 31-35
　　Prediction Of Judas' Betrayal And Peter's Denial

Silent Confession

Prayer Of Confession
Merciful God, we have not loved you with all our heart and mind and strength and soul. Lord have mercy.
Lord have mercy.
We have not loved our neighbors as you have taught us. Christ have mercy.
Christ have mercy.
We have not fully received the saving grace of your word and life. Lord have mercy.
Lord have mercy.
May the Lord have mercy upon you, forgive and heal you by his steadfast love made known to us by the passion, death, and resurrection of Jesus Christ our Lord.
Amen. Thanks be to God.

Meditation

Scripture Reading   Matthew 26:26-29
 Institution Of The Last Supper

The Prayer Of Great Thanksgiving

The Distribution Of The Elements
This evening we will be sharing in the Lord's Supper one table at a time. You are asked to come to the Lord's table at the direction of the ushers.

Communion Hymns
 "I Come With Joy" (People, Song Sheet)
 "Let Us Break Bread Together" (People, Song Sheet)
 "Now The Silence" (Choir)
 "One Bread, One Body" (People, Song Sheet)
 "What Wondrous Love Is This?" (People, Song Sheet)
 "Take Our Bread" (People, Song Sheet)
 "Because Thou Hast Said" (Choir)
 "For The Bread Which You Have Broken" (People, Song Sheet)

Scripture Reading Matthew 26:30, 36-46
Mount Of Olives And The Garden Of Gethsemane

Prayer
God in heaven, who, through your Son, has paid a high price for our forgiveness, symbolized by our elements of bread and wine: Inspire us to rid all uncleanness from our lives in thanksgiving for the redemption that your Son gives. In his name we pray. Amen.

To Be Continued ...

Good Friday

The climax for examining the areas of our lives where we may be wounded individually as well as corporately is Good Friday. An especially meaningful and moving way to bring this portion of *Wounded For Us* to a close is with a Tenebrae service that has been adapted to include the five wounds of Christ. The sample Tenebrae service comes from the Crescent Avenue United Methodist Church and is a continuation of the Maundy Thursday service. Following the Tenebrae service is a community Good Friday service that was sponsored by the East Noble Ministerial Association that used as its focus the five wounds of Christ.

The Tenebrae service begins with a greeting that comes from John 3:18, 19. The opening hymn is the first stanza of "Were You There?" In this service, rather than listing the stanza of each of the verses to be sung, the words are printed. The anthems noted are those that were used by the chancel choir of the Crescent Avenue Church. Churches using *Wounded for Us* will want to choose their own hymns and special music.

The first major section of the service, "The Passion Of Our Lord," picks up where the Maundy Thursday service left off. Its focus is the arrest and trial of Jesus. The second major section, "The First Four Wounds Of Christ," as well as the third section, "Seven Last Words," recount Jesus' agony on the cross. As the appropriate verse of "Were You There?" is sung, one of the Lenten candles should be extinguished. In this service, Jesus being pierced in the side has been moved from the second wound to the fifth wound. The order for the wounds during the first five weeks of Lent follow a progression that was dictated by how we are wounded. The order for the Tenebrae service is dictated by how Jesus was wounded.

The readings for the seven last words of Jesus from the cross can come directly from the scriptures or may be adapted from standard Tenebrae service readings. Following each reading a candle should be extinguished. A seven-light candelabra works well for this purpose. At this point in the service the process of turning off the lights in the sanctuary should begin. The result then is that following the reading of the seventh word the church is in nearly complete darkness.

The death of Jesus is the focus of the fourth section of the service with the final section dealing with the response of those who were there the first Good Friday as well as those who are a part of the congregation. When the final Lenten candle is extinguished during the singing of "Were You There?" enough light should remain for the stripping of the church in the final section. If a Lenten wreath has been used with a center black candle for Good Friday, it should be extinguished following the stripping of the church. For the reading from Isaiah 53:4-9, the final verse of "Were You There?" and the dismissal the sanctuary should be given in total darkness. In the service, the choir sings the final verses. When the service was used at Crescent Avenue the choir had helped with the stripping of the church, taking their items to the back of the church. Following the dismissal, enough lights should be turned on to allow the people to safely leave the sanctuary.

The community Good Friday service assumes a wide participation by the pastors of the community. Different pastors are assigned to give a short meditation on each of the five wounds. Other pastors serve as liturgists. Special music may be added or substituted for the suggested hymns. Good Friday candles could be lighted instead of being extinguished.

Tenebrae Worship Service

Good Friday

Prelude

Greeting
And this is the judgment, that the light came into the world, and we loved darkness rather than light.
God is light, in whom there is no darkness at all.
For God sent his Son into the world, not to condemn the world, but that the world might be saved through him.
Come, let us worship in spirit and in truth.

Lenten Hymn "Were You There?"
(... when they crucified my Lord)

Opening Prayer
The Lord be with you.
And also with you.
Let us pray:
Most gracious God, look with mercy upon your family gathered here for whom our Lord Jesus Christ was wounded and betrayed, given into sinful hands, and suffered death upon the cross. Strengthen our faith and forgive our betrayals as we enter the way of his passion; through him who lives and reigns with you and the Holy Spirit forever and ever. Amen.

The Passion Of Our Lord
Hymn "Go To Dark Gethsemane"

Scripture Reading Matthew 26:47-55
Jesus Arrested

Anthem "O Love, How Deep"

Scripture Reading   Matthew 26:57-69
    Jesus Before The Sanhedrin

Anthem   "To Mock Your Reign, O Dearest Lord"

Scripture Reading   Matthew 26:69-75
    Peter Denies Jesus

Hymn   "O Sacred Head Now Wounded"

First Four Wounds Of Christ

First Wound Scripture Reading   Matthew 27:26
    Wounded On The Back

Hymn   "Were You There?"
               (... when they scourged him on the back)
(Extinguish a Lenten candle)

Second Wound Scripture Reading   Matthew 27:28-31
    Wounded On The Head

Hymn   "Were You There?"
               (... when they crowned him with the thorns)
(Extinguish a Lenten candle)

Third Wound Scripture Reading   Matthew 27:32-34
    Wounded On the Hands

Hymn   "Were You There?"
               (... when they nailed him to the tree)
(Extinguish a Lenten candle)

Fourth Wound Scripture Reading   John 19:16-18
    Wounded On The Feet

Hymn "Were You There?"
(... when they nailed him to the tree)
(Extinguish a Lenten candle)

Seven Last Words

First Word Luke 23:32-34
"Father, forgive them; for they know not what they do."
(Extinguish one of the candelabra candles)

Second Word Luke 23:39-43
"Today, you will be with me in paradise."
(Extinguish one of the candelabra candles)

Third Word John 19:25-27
"Woman, behold your son! ... Behold your mother!"
(Extinguish one of the candelabra candles)

Fourth Word Matthew 27:45-47
"My God, my God, why hast thou forsaken me?"
(Extinguish one of the candelabra candles)

Fifth Word John 19:28
"I thirst."
(Extinguish one of the candelabra candles)

Sixth Word John 19:29, 30
"It is finished."
(Extinguish one of the candelabra candles)

Seventh Word Luke 23:44-47
"Father, into thy hands I commit my Spirit!"
(Extinguish one of the candelabra candles)

The Fifth Wound Of Christ
Fifth Wound Scripture Reading   John 19:33-34
     Wounded In The Side

Hymn   "Were You There?"
(... when they pierced him in the side)
(Extinguish final Lenten candle)

Response To The Death Of Christ
Scripture Reading   Matthew 27:51-61
     Death And Burial Of Jesus

Hymn   "Were You There?"
(... when the sun refused to shine)

Stripping Of The Church
(Extinguish Good Friday candle, church in total darkness)

Scripture Reading   Isaiah 53:4-9
     Jesus, The Suffering Servant

Anthem   "Were You There?"
(... when they laid him in the tomb)

Dismissal

Going Forth

(Tell the people they are welcome to stay and meditate)

To Be Continued ...

Community Worship Service

Good Friday Service

Prelude

Call To Worship   Hebrews 4:15, 16; Isaiah 53:5
For we do not have a high priest who is unable to sympathize with our weakness,
> **but we have one who in every respect has been tested as we are, yet without sin.**

He was wounded for our transgressions, crushed for our iniquities;
> **upon him was the punishment that made us whole, and by his bruises we are healed.**

Let us therefore approach the throne of grace with boldness,
> **so that we may receive mercy and find grace to help in time of need.**

Hymn   "Beneath The Cross Of Jesus"

Responsive Reading
Wounded for us, wounded for us, there on the cross he was wounded for us; gone are our transgressions, and now we are free, all because Jesus was wounded for us.
> **Dying for me, dying for me, there on the cross he was dying for me; now in his death my redemption I see, all because Jesus was dying for me.**

Risen for us, risen for us, up from the grave he was risen for us; now evermore from death's sting we are free, all because Jesus has risen for us.
> **Living for me, living for me, up to the skies he is living for me; daily he's pleading and praying for me, O how I praise him, he's living for me.**

The Lord's Prayer   (Ecumenical text)

Offering
- **Offertory Sentence**
  [Jesus said] "Truly, I say to you, as you did it to one of the least of these [my brothers and sisters], you did it to me" (Matthew 25:40).
- **Offertory**
- **Doxology**
- **Prayer Of Consecration**

The First Wound Of Christ
The Back — Wounded In Our Hopes And Dreams

So he released Barabbas for them; and after flogging Jesus, he handed him over to be crucified (Matthew 27:26).

Meditation

Lighting Of The First Good Friday Candle
- **Hymn**   "Were You There?"
  (... when they scourged him on the back)

Prayer

Dear God, we light the first Good Friday candle as a reminder of Christ being wounded on the back. It is also a symbol of the places in our lives where we are wounded in our hopes and in our dreams. Take upon yourself the wounds we bring that you might redeem and resurrect them, that we might be set free from the wounds that bind us, to a life of everlasting joy and peace. Amen.

The Second Wound Of Christ
The Head — Wounded In Our Thoughts

They stripped him and put a scarlet robe on him, and after twisting some thorns into a crown, they put it on his head. They put a reed in his right hand and knelt before him and mocked him, saying, "Hail, King of the Jews!" They spat on him, and took the reed and struck him on the head (Matthew 27:28-31).

Meditation

Lighting Of The Second Good Friday Candle
    Hymn   "Were You There?"
        (... when they crowned him with the thorns)

Prayer
Dear God, we light the second Good Friday candle as a reminder that Christ was wounded on the head by the crown of thorns. It is also a symbol of the places in our lives where we are wounded because of our thoughts. Take upon yourself the wounds we bring that you might redeem and resurrect them, that we might be set free from the wounds that bind us, to a life of everlasting joy and peace. Amen.

The Third Wound Of Christ
The Hands — Wounded In Our Relationships

As they went out, they came upon a man from Cyrene named Simon; they compelled this man to carry his cross. And when they came to a place called Golgotha (which means Place of a Skull), they offered him wine to drink, mixed with gall; but when he tasted it, he would not drink (Matthew 27:32-34).

Meditation

Lighting Of The Third Good Friday Candle
    Hymn   "Were You There?"
        (... when they nailed him to the tree)

Prayer
Dear God, we light the third Good Friday candle as a reminder that Christ was wounded on the hands by the nails of the cross. It is also a symbol of where we are wounded because of the places in our lives where our relationships with others are broken. Take upon yourself the wounds we bring that you might redeem and resurrect them, that we might be set free from the wounds that bind us, to a life of everlasting joy and peace. Amen.

Hymn "Jesus, Keep Me Near The Cross"

The Fourth Wound Of Christ
The Feet — Wounded In Our Actions

And when they had crucified him, they divided his clothes among themselves by casting lots; then they sat down there and kept watch over him. Over his head they put the charge against him, which read, "This is Jesus, the King of the Jews" (Matthew 27:35-38).

Meditation

Lighting Of The Fourth Good Friday Candle
Hymn "Were You There?"
(... when they nailed him to the tree)

Prayer

Dear God, we light the fourth Good Friday candle as a reminder that Christ was wounded on the feet by the nails of the cross. It is also a symbol of the places in our lives where we are wounded because of our actions or the actions of others. Take upon yourself the wounds we bring that you might redeem and resurrect them, that we might be set free from these binding wounds, to a life of everlasting joy and peace. Amen.

Solo "You Are The Christ"

The Fifth Wound Of Christ
The Side — Wounded In Our Spirit And Emotions

But when they came to Jesus and saw that he was already dead, they did not break his legs. Instead, one of the soldiers pierced his side with a spear, and at once blood and water came out (John 19:33-34).

Meditation

Lighting Of The Fifth Good Friday Candle
Hymn "Were You There?"
(... when they pierced him in the side)

Prayer

Dear God, we light the fifth Good Friday candle as a reminder that Christ was wounded in the side by the spear. It is also a symbol of the places in our lives where we are wounded in our spirit and our emotions. Christ take upon yourself the wounds we bring that you might redeem and resurrect them, that we might be set free from these binding wounds, to a life of everlasting joy and peace. Amen.

Closing Hymn "In The Cross Of Christ I Glory"

Dismissal With Blessing

Anthem "On Yonder Cross"

(Tell the people they are encouraged to depart in silence to ponder what it means that Jesus was wounded for us.)

To Be Continued ...

Easter Sunday

The six Sundays in Lent have been a precursor for the coming of Easter. During each of these "little Easters" the healing power of Jesus' victory over the grave and his being raised from the dead has been proclaimed and experienced. Now it is time to experience the power of the resurrection in its fullness. Friday night, the Tenebrae service was filled with a sense of grief, despair, and hopelessness, and those attending left a bare and dark sanctuary. The first Easter, the women who came to the tomb to attend to the body of Jesus arrived with heavy hearts. But, these feelings were very quickly turned to amazement and wonderment as they found the stone to the tomb rolled away and the body of their Lord gone.

One way to help those attending worship on Easter Sunday to experience the women's reversal of feelings is by having the sanctuary dark as the people arrive, just as it was left at the end of the Tenebrae service. The first act of worship is the proclamation "Christ is risen" to which the people respond, "Christ is risen, indeed." The lights are turned on and a glorious processional hymn begins. As the hymn is sung, the paraments are returned to their rightful place, the Easter flowers are brought in, and the Lenten wreath is replaced by an Easter wreath. At this time the altar candles as well as the Christ candle are lighted. The remaining candles in the Easter wreath are lighted later in the service.

The Easter worship service that follows, begins with a darkened sanctuary and climaxes with the lighting of the candles on the Easter wreath. The theme for the service is taken from the hymn, "To God Be The Glory." Churches using this service will want to adapt it to their own Easter customs. The service assumes that there was an Ash Wednesday service at which time the purple candles for the Lenten wreath were introduced. An Easter sermon has been provided, complete with sermon notes.

Worship Service

Easter Sunday

To God Be The Glory

Proclamation
    Christ is risen!
    Christ is risen, indeed!

Hymn   "Christ The Lord Is Risen Today"

Reading From The Psalter   Psalm 118:14-29

Announcements

Special Music

Reading From The History Of The Church   Acts 10:34-43

Epistle Reading   Colossians 3:1-4

Hymn   "Low In The Grave"

Gospel Lesson   Matthew 28:1-10

Offering

Sermon   "Healed"

Lighting Of The Easter Candles

First Candle: Healed In Our Thoughts
    As on Ash Wednesday when we brought a purple candle for the places in our lives where we are wounded in our thoughts, so now we bring a white candle as a symbol of where the redeeming power of Christ and the work of the Holy Spirit have renewed the places where we have been wounded in our thinking.

Hymn "My Tribute"

Second Candle: Healed In Our Spirit And Emotions
As on Ash Wednesday when we brought a purple candle for the places in our lives where we are wounded in our spirit and emotions, so now we bring a white candle as a symbol of where the redeeming power of Christ and the work of the Holy Spirit have invited us to let go and let God.

Hymn "My Tribute"

Third Candle: Healed In Our Hopes And Dreams
As on Ash Wednesday when we brought a purple candle for the places in our lives where we are wounded in our hopes and dreams, so now we bring a white candle as a symbol of where the redeeming power of Christ and the work of the Holy Spirit has brought hope and new beginnings.

Hymn "My Tribute"

Fourth Candle: Healed In Our Relationships
As on Ash Wednesday when we brought a purple candle for the places in our lives where we have experienced broken relationships, destructive relationships, or the fear of relationships, so now we bring a white candle as a symbol of where the redeeming power of Christ and the work of the Holy Spirit has brought new and healthy reconciliation.

Hymn "My Tribute"

Fifth Candle: Healed In Our Actions
As on Ash Wednesday when we brought a purple candle for the places in our lives where we were wounded in our actions, so now we bring a white candle as a symbol of where the redeeming power of Christ and the work of the Holy Spirit has brought forgiveness for past actions and will help to prevent destructive actions in the future.

Hymn "My Tribute"

Sixth Candle: The New Jerusalem
As on Ash Wednesday when we brought a purple candle to symbolize the places where Jerusalem and the cities of the world are wounded, so now we bring a white candle as a symbol of the kingdom of God breaking into our midst.

Prayer Of Thanksgiving
Our Father, we give you thanks that on the cross your Son took upon himself the places in our lives where we are wounded. Today, we rejoice and give thanks that he triumphed over the grave, bringing healing and wholeness. Help us this day to celebrate the places where you have brought healing and new beginnings in our lives by the power that you demonstrated the first Easter. Amen.

Hymn "This Is A Day Of New Beginnings"

Sending Forth
This is a day of new beginnings,
Time to remember and move on,
Time to believe what love is bringing,
Laying to rest the pain that's gone.*

Congregational Benediction "I Serve A Risen Savior"
(vs. 1, 2)

Postlude

---

*Taken from "This Is A Day Of New Beginnings," by Brian Wren © 1983, 1987, Hope Publishing Co., Carol Stream, Illinois 60188. All rights reserved. Used by permission. Permission to reproduce these words must be obtained from Hope Publishing Co., 800-323-1049, www.hopepublishing.com.

Bulletin Insert

Easter Sunday

Healed

Matthew 28:1-10

Sermon Notes
This Is A Day Of New Beginnings
See, I am making all things new. — Revelation 21:5a

This is a day of new beginnings,
Time to remember and move on,
Time to believe what love is bringing
Laying to rest the pain that's gone.

For by the life and death of Jesus,
Love's mighty Spirit, now as then,
Can make for us a world of difference,
As faith and hope are born again. *

Transformation

Bulbs	Flower
Seed	Apple Tree
Cocoons	Butterflies
Winter	Spring
End	Beginning
Time	Infinity
Doubt	Believing
Life	Eternity
Death	Resurrection

Healed
- **Thoughts**
  Minds renewed so that we might discern what is good and acceptable to God.

- **Spirit And Emotions**
  Invited to let go and let God.

- **Hope And Dreams**
  Create new beginnings.

- **Relationships**
  Reconciliation with God, with self, and with neighbor.

- **Actions**
  When wounded in our actions call out to God for help.
  Ask God to prevent us from making poor decisions.

- **Jerusalem**
  Experience the kingdom of God breaking into our midst.

---

*Taken from "This Is A Day Of New Beginnings," by Brian Wren © 1983, 1987, Hope Publishing Co., Carol Stream, Illinois 60188. All rights reserved. Used by permission. Permission to reproduce these words must be obtained from Hope Publishing Co., 800-323-1049, www.hopepublishing.com.

Sermon

Healed
Matthew 28:1-10

When I was a student at Perkins School of Theology in the '60s, one of the two preaching professors was the Reverend Ronald Sleeth. His wife, Natalie, was, and still is, an accomplished composer of Christian music. Much of what she has written is for children. However, one of her hymns for adults is to be found in the *United Methodist Hymnal*, 707, "Hymn Of Promise."

The "Hymn Of Promise" is about transformation. A bulb is transformed into a flower; a seed into an apple tree; a cocoon into a butterfly; winter into spring. During this Lenten season, we have also been talking about transformation. Because of his death on the cross, Christ can take upon himself the places that we are wounded and can transform them into something beautiful.

Thoughts
We have seen how Christ can take the places that we are wounded in our thoughts because of the content of our minds, and invite us to be transformed by the renewing of our minds so that we might discern what is the will of God — what is good and acceptable and perfect (Romans 12:2).

Spirit And Emotions
We have seen how Christ can take the places in our lives where we are wounded in spirit and emotions and invites us to let them go and let God.

Hope And Dreams
We have seen how Christ can take the places in our lives where we have been wounded in our hopes and dreams and create new beginnings. He listens to our pain, walks with us for a while, and then helps us create a new future.

Relationships
We have seen how Christ can take the places in our lives where we have been wounded in our relationships and help us to be reconciled to him, to ourselves, and our neighbor.

Actions
We have seen how Christ can take the places in our lives where we have been wounded in our actions and would invite us to call out to him for his help to save us.

Jerusalem
We have seen how Christ rode into a wounded city that first Palm Sunday. Jerusalem is still a wounded city and we look forward with eager longing until that day when the New Jerusalem would descend and the kingdom of God might reign. In the in-between time we have been given a taste of the heavenly banquet each time we gather to partake of the bread and fruit of the vine at communion.

One of the minor inconsistencies to be found in the accounts of the first Easter in the four gospels is that in our lesson for this morning the women take hold of Jesus' feet, while in John, Mary is told specifically not to touch him. However, one might try to reconcile these two positions, one point seems clear, the body of Jesus went through a transformation following his death on the cross. His resurrection was not a matter of the restoration of the old, but the beginning of something new.

When we are wounded, for whatever reason, life can never be as it once was. The world has forever changed. We may long for the good old days, but they are never coming back. The end of the old should not be a reason for despair for the future. And the reason? God is continually making all things new. In the first verse of her hymn, Natalie Sleeth has helped us to see this miracle in nature. In the third verse, she puts this truth within the context of each of our lives. "In our end is our beginning; in our time infinity, in our doubt there is believing, in our life, eternity. In our death, a resurrection; at the last a victory, unrevealed until its season, something God alone can see." *

For Christians every day has the possibility of being a new day, a new beginning. This is especially true for today, Easter. It is a celebration of the good news that following death there is the possibility of resurrection. Brian Wren, an English composer, wrote a hymn in 1978 which puts well how God's Easter transforming power can create new beginnings when we have been wounded.

This is a day of new beginnings,
Time to remember and move on,
Time to believe what love is bringing,
Laying to rest the pain that's gone.

For by the life and death of Jesus,
Love's mighty Spirit now as then,
Can make for us a world of difference,
As faith and hope are born again.

Then let us, with the Spirit's daring,
Step from the past and leave behind
Our disappointment, guilt, and grieving;
Seeking new paths, and sure to find.

Christ is alive, and goes before us
To show and share what love can do.
This is a day of new beginnings;
Our God is making all things new.**

This morning, our Lenten wreath has been transformed into an Easter wreath. The five purple candles and the one black candle have been replaced by six white candles. In the center of the wreath is an additional large white candle, the Christ candle. This center candle represents Christ's victory over sin and death. From it we will be lighting the six white candles to symbolize how the redemptive power of Christ being wounded on the cross can heal our wounds.

This is a day of new beginnings. This is a day to experience the transforming power of the resurrection to heal our wounds.

*Taken from "Hymn Of Praise" by Natalie Sleeth, © 1986, Hope Publishing Co., Carol Stream, Illinois 60188. All rights reserved. Used by permission. Permission to reproduce these words must be obtained from Hope Publishing Co., 800-323-1049, www.hopepublishing.com.

**Taken from "This Is A Day Of New Beginnings," by Brian Wren © 1983, 1987, Hope Publishing Co., Carol Stream, Illinois 60188. All rights reserved. Used by permission. Permission to reproduce these words must be obtained from Hope Publishing Co., 800-323-1049, www.hopepublishing.com.

Visuals

Candles

Five Crosses, Five Candles

The simplest visual for the Lenten candles is the one Crescent Avenue used the first time *Wounded For Us* was presented. Five votive candles were placed in front of the five crosses that were engraved on the reredos of the altar. Since most churches are not fortunate enough to have this type of altar, the five candles may be placed in front of five crosses that have been placed on the altar or some other convenient place in the sanctuary. The type of candle used is somewhat dependent upon the size of crosses employed. An adaptation of this arrangement would be to use five crucifixes for Lent and five crosses for Easter.

Lenten Wreath/Easter Wreath

A Lenten wreath can easily be made by obtaining a round form from any craft store, placing holders in it for the candles, and then decorating it with dried grapevine or other dark branches for Lent and bright flowers or greenery for Easter (can either be artificial or real). During the Lenten season a large, black candle may be placed in the center of the wreath to be replaced with a white candle on Easter Sunday. From experience the most difficult part of this construction is to find candleholders the same size as the candles being used.

A Lenten wreath works well for up to six candles: six Sundays in Lent with a black candle in the center for Good Friday. If one wanted to include a candle for Maundy Thursday, a seven-branch candelabra might work well with a separate black candle for Good Friday. Another option would be to construct a rising circular wreath that could accommodate up to seven candles. It could be decorated in a fashion similar to the wreaths described above.

An Easter wreath replaces the five purple candles and one black candle with six white candles. The Christ candle is placed in the center. These are decorated with bright flowers and greenery.

Display

In my second appointment I was very fortunate to have a lady who constructed wonderful displays to illustrate the emphasis for a particular service or season of the church year. For *Wounded For Us*, a church may want to consider having a different display for each of the Sundays in Lent or a display to which additions would be made each Sunday. The obvious elements for such displays would be a crown of thorns, a spear, a whip, and nails. For Palm Sunday a church might want to include something that either represents Jerusalem or its own setting.

Another direction for a display would be to focus on how we are wounded. Week One, a display could be created that would illustrate the ways that we may be wounded in our thoughts. Week Two, the display from week one may be replaced with one that represents how we are wounded in spirit and emotions. For those churches with adequate space, the display for the emphasis for a particular week could be placed in a prominent place in the sanctuary with the previous displays being moved to another location in the sanctuary.

Today, many church sanctuaries are equipped with the technology that allows for the projection of visuals. This possibility offers a wonderful opportunity to visually reinforce each week's emphasis. It is left to each church's creative team to develop such resources.

Handouts

One option to help reinforce the themes for each Sunday would be to give those attending the services something to take home with them. Since Sermon Notes are provided on the Bulletin Insert that emphasize the place where we are wounded, this additional handout may well want to focus on the place where Jesus was wounded. Classes or groups in the church may be recruited to help with the production of these reminders.

Two obvious handouts would be nails for the fourth and fifth Sundays in Lent and Palm crosses for Palm Sunday. For the first

Sunday, small crowns of thorn could be distributed. A blunt spear could be given out the second Sunday, and small whips the third.

Bulletins

If you design your own bulletin covers, there are specific visuals that will help to emphasize the program.

Week One: a crown of thorns in the upper left corner
Week Two: add a spear in the lower right corner
Week Three: add a whip in the lower left corner
Week Four and Five: add nails in the upper right corner
Palm Sunday: depict the parade of palms in the center of the above visuals
Easter: continue the visuals with a barren cross and lilies in the center instead of the palms